D0385188

The You That Could Be

The You That _Could_ Be

Dr. Fitzhugh Dodson

FOLLETT PUBLISHING COMPANY
CHICAGO

Copyright © 1976 by Dr. Fitzhugh Dodson. All rights reserved. No part of this publication may be reproduced, stored in a retrieval system or transmitted in any form or by any means, electronic, mechanical, photocopying, recording, or otherwise, without the prior permission of the publisher. Manufactured in the United States of America.

Library of Congress Catalog Card Number: 75-5202
ISBN: 0-695-80606-8

First Printing

To Cecilia
with love

Contents

Acknowledgments

To these people, my special thanks:

Every time I write a book I am once again impressed that I am standing on the shoulders of many people who have contributed in one way or another to the completion of the book.

I am grateful to the many behavioral scientists all over the world upon whose experimental and clinical research I have drawn. As in my previous writings, I have chosen not to clutter up the book with footnotes and scholarly references. But my gratitude remains the same.

I am also grateful for what I have learned about both the Potential Self and the Repressive Self from more than twenty years of clinical practice with my patients: adults, adolescents, and children. It is a rare patient who does not teach me something new.

I want also to express my sincere thanks to those who have been especially helpful in the writing and editing of the book. Paula Reuben collaborated in the writing of the book, and she is not only an excellent and versatile writer but a delight to work with. Jeanne Harris, whose editorial assistance with my previous books *How To Parent* and *How To Father* was of enormous help to me, once again has earned the gratitude of every reader. If the book flows easily and smoothly, it is in large measure due to Jeanne's editorial blue pencil. In addition, my sincere thanks go to my editor at Follett, John Hess, himself a skilled writer, and to Vytautas Babusis, his associate, for their help and editorial suggestions. And to Jenny Gumpertz, who also aided in no small measure with her skillful editorial work on the manuscript.

I also want to express my thanks to all who have enabled the original rough manuscript to grow into the completed book, particularly to my daughter Robin Dodson and to Robert Giorgi. Also to Chris Ratajack, Lani Stewart, and Chris and Susan Liles for reading the original early drafts of the manuscript and making suggestions for changes.

Acknowledgments

I also want to say thanks to lecture audiences in many different parts of the country who have heard part of this material and helped me indirectly by their audience response to shape it into publication in book form.

Finally, to my secretary Lee Morris, for all of the varied duties she performed in helping the early rough draft grow into the completed manuscript.

I am deeply grateful to all of these people. Without them, I could not have written this book.

Fitzhugh Dodson
Redondo Beach, California
Summer, 1975

The You That Could Be

1. Your Hidden Self

Is this a reasonably accurate picture of you?

You are full of zest and enthusiasm for life. You are spontaneous and outgoing. You have no fears of trying new things. You are not worried about what others think of you. You are able to express the full range of all your feelings: joy, excitement, love, fear, sadness, and anger. You have a deep capacity for intimacy and closeness, and you are able to love and be loved in return. You have an enormous curiosity about the world and a powerful drive to learn all you can about it. Your self-confidence is solid and secure. You are not anxious or depressed; instead you have a hearty, rollicking, sensuous enjoyment of life.

You may be thinking: "No, that doesn't describe me, but I sure wish it did!" Or you may feel: "That only describes part of me, but I'd gladly give a year's salary if it described all of me!"

Would you be surprised to learn that there was a time in your life when this personality picture *was* an accurate description of you? What I have been describing is your Potential Self. And there was a time in your life when you were fully using your Potential Self. When you were a young toddler, about a year old, you were exactly like the personality picture I have just sketched.

In fact, *all* toddlers possess these personality characteristics. But what happens? Our society (parents, relatives, neighbors, school) grabs ahold of these spontaneous, loving, self-confident toddlers and teaches them fears, worries, and inhibitions, erodes their self-confidence, and makes them into caricatures of the persons they could be. The Potential Self becomes imprisoned by the Repressive Self.

The message of this book is that you were once fully utilizing your Potential Self and that you can learn how to do it again. That joyous, spontaneous, loving, self-confident Potential Self still lives within you and is trying to break loose from the chains with which he or she is bound.

Your Potential Self is the *you that could be,* the unique bundle of personality potentialities you were born with.

Your particular combination of genes never before existed on this planet and will never exist again. Your fingerprints are unique, unmatched by anyone else of all the teeming millions of people on earth. Your personality is also unique. *There is not a single individual in the entire world whose personality is like yours.* Stop a minute and think about that last sentence; it is a true and very powerful statement.

The best analogy I can think of to get across the uniqueness of your personality is for you to imagine that you were born an absolutely unique combination of colors. No other human being anywhere in the world has your individual and beautiful color scheme. But then our society, which is afraid of allowing people to express their individuality, has a succession of people (parents, relatives, teachers, etc.) paint you a dull dead gray so that your own individual color pattern is covered up.

Now let me move from that imaginative metaphor to very down-to-earth psychological facts. What does it mean to you, that society has painted over your own unique colors with a dull, dead gray, that society has covered up your Potential Self with a rigid and tyrannical Repressive Self?

It means, for one thing, *you are using only one-third of your potential talents and abilities.*

One-third. That's what I said.

If society had left your Potential Self alone when you were a year old, you would be using all of your Potential Self now instead of a third of it. But instead, your Potential Self is handicapped at every turn by your other self, your Repressive Self.

Even our everyday speech shows we unconsciously recognize that we have more than one self. For example, you may get up some morning feeling grouchy and irritable and snarl at your family. Afterwards you feel badly about it and apologize by saying: "You'll have to forgive me. I guess I'm not myself today." This implies that there is a potential (better) self which you failed to live up to that particular morning.

Shakespeare said the same thing in a little more flowery language when he had one of his characters, Polonius, advise his son:

"This above all: to thine own self be true,
And it must follow, as the night the day,
Thou canst not then be false to any man."

Here again is the idea that there is a Potential Self to which we should be true.

The Repressive Self, on the other hand, is the self which restricts us. How often have you said, "I'm all tied up in knots," or you attended a party where you didn't know many of the other guests and were a little ill at ease? Later, looking back on it, you remarked: "I guess I was pretty *self*-conscious." Here the "self" you are referring to is a *different* kind of self. To be conscious of, or true to, this "self" is not a good thing, because this is the one that represses you.

Your Repressor is not hard to recognize once you know it's there. How many times have you said: "I can't do it because . . .

"I've never tried that before.

"It's hard for me to express myself.

"I get nervous even thinking about it.

"I'm not sure I'd be doing the right thing.

"I'm afraid I'll make a fool of myself."

These are all examples of your Repressive Self, keeping you from expressing your true Potential Self.

I know a great deal about these two selves, partly because I have spent over twenty years as a psychologist helping people break free of their Repressive Selves and develop their Potential Selves; and partly because I have struggled to become free from my own Repressor to find my own Potential. Let me tell you a story about myself that goes back many years.

Years ago, as a freshman in high school, I was

quite impressed by our school newspaper, *The Collegian.* This paper had won all sorts of high school national press honors. I thought the students who wrote the articles and published the paper were supermen, far above an ordinary high school student like myself.

In my freshman year I happened to take a journalism course. Actually, I had no passionate interest in journalism, but one of my friends had told me it was easier than the regular English course.

My best friend, Gene, was also taking journalism. He tried out for the newspaper, made it, and kept urging and prodding me to try out too.

"Gene," I told him, "you're crazy. I can't do anything like that. I've never written a news story in my life. I just know I can't do it. Let's face it, pal. I don't have the talent."

But Gene was persistent, and he finally talked me into it.

Sports interested me the most at that time. So, after hemming, hawing, and stalling as long as possible, I finally took action, mostly to get Gene off my back. I went to see the sports editor and asked him if there was an opening in his department. I assumed he would give me a big writing test or something like that to qualify. Much to my surprise, all he said was: "You can cover the sophomore basketball team. The first game is next Tuesday."

I traveled to the opposite end of town to cover the first game, wrote it up the way they had taught me in journalism class, and handed it in to the editor the day after the game.

And by George, when the paper came out the following week, there was my story!

Of course, it was only a few paragraphs and the editor had changed all but about four or five of my original words; but, nevertheless—it was *my* story! I wheedled about sixteen copies of the paper and passed them out to my friends. I felt a glow of journalistic pride every time I read, reread, and reread that tiny story. Because it was *mine*, the first of its kind I had ever done.

I continued covering the sophomore basketball team that season. To my amazement, in the spring when appointments for the following year's staff were announced, I was promoted to assistant sports editor.

By the time I graduated from high school I was associate editor of the paper, one step below editor-in-chief. And who was editor-in-chief? My friend Gene, who had convinced me I *could* write for the paper.

The reason I am telling you this story is simple. If anyone had told me when I entered high school as a green freshman: "By the time you graduate, you're going to be associate editor of that award-winning school paper," I would have thought he was just plain crazy. Because I felt I wasn't good enough.

And the point is: I would have been 100 percent wrong about myself!

I would have sadly underestimated myself, underestimated a talent I actually possessed but wasn't aware of. It took someone else to convince me, and he had to work mighty hard to do it. If Gene hadn't talked me into applying for the job, chances are I would never have discovered I had any writing skills. And that means I would never in a million years have written this book you are reading now.

What Gene did for me I'm going to try to do for you. I hope to put you in touch with that one-year-old you once were, who has been trying to break free of the chains society has put upon him or her, that Potential Self you do not know you have. For your Potential Self contains a variety of talents and abilities you don't even dream you possess. These talents and abilities are untapped and undeveloped.

For instance, you have within yourself the self-confidence to try new things, the knack of making and holding new friends, the ability to stand up for yourself and say no to people when that is necessary. You have the capacity for a full and uninhibited enjoyment of sensuality and sexuality, the ability to be popular, to work with people, to plan and direct the activities of groups, to attract people to you. You are capable of expressing yourself in all sorts of interesting and creative activities, of using some special talents which are as yet undeveloped within you, such as art or writing or music or sports. *But you are almost totally unaware that you have these hidden capacities!*

A former patient of mine illustrates this point perfectly. She came to me originally for marriage counseling, because the conflicts between her and her husband had become almost intolerable. Her husband was a domineering tyrant who was almost wholly unaware that he was so domineering. She had played the role of doormat in the marriage for seventeen years until something within her finally rebelled. I began working with them, seeing each one separately, to help them confront the conflicts which were tearing their marriage apart.

About three months after she had first begun therapy, the wife arrived one day for her appointment and announced she had decided to experiment with oil painting. I encouraged her to give it a try. I want you to realize that this was a forty-two-year-old woman who had never been interested in art before and had never studied anything related to art in school. Now suddenly, as she was struggling

23

to get free from her Repressor and find the psychological strength to stand up to her husband, an interest in expressing herself through art had erupted
somewhere within the depths of her being.

She bought an oil-painting set. Since she lived
near the ocean, she began at first to paint the sea.
Her paintings were amazingly good, especially
when you consider she had no experience with art
and no professional training.

The seas in her early paintings were wild and
turbulent. Then slowly she began to have the courage to stand up to her husband and their conflicts
began to be resolved. She was getting in touch with
the self-confidence and calm assertiveness of her
Potential Self. As these psychological changes took
place in her, the seas in her paintings began to
change from stormy and turbulent to calm and
peaceful. This symbolized beautifully the beginning of a calm inner confidence as she started to
discover and use her Potential.

Now I want to remind you that I was this
woman's therapist, and my purpose was not to help
her become an artist or to bring out her repressed
artistic side. She came to me for marriage counseling. My goal was to help her work out the problems that were tormenting her in marriage. In order to do this, I needed to help her gain freedom

from her Repressor and discover the power of her Potential Self. As her therapy gave her the courage to break free from her Repressive Self, she not only learned to stand up to her husband, but she was enabled to get in touch with an artistic side of herself which had lain dormant and untapped for forty-two years.

This is why it is important for you to know something about psychology. Psychologists have studied the hidden abilities of people such as this woman and you yourself have. What's more, psychology has determined some of the reasons that prevent you from developing your potentialities.

You may be asking yourself right now: "Well, if I have all of these unused talents and potentialities, what prevents me from using them?"

The answer, of course, is our old villain: the Repressive Self.

Here are two examples of how your Repressive Self works, blocking you from using the hidden talents and abilities of your Potential Self.

Suppose I asked you to walk across a one-foot wide board on the ground. I don't think you would have any particular difficulty.

However, suppose that now we walk over to the construction site of a building. The same board is placed on a scaffolding twenty feet in the air and you are asked to walk across it. It's the same board. The exact same width. It's the same "you." You've already shown you can do it easily. You walked across it on the ground. What happens twenty feet up? You look over the side and see the ground far below. You are apprehensive and perhaps even a little panicky. Why? Your Repressor is whispering things in your ear. Things like: "Oh sure, you did it when you were on the ground, but how do you know you can do it up in the air? And what would happen if you fell? It's all pretty risky; you'd be a fool to chance it."

Another illustration: you could learn to give a good speech before an audience of 300 people.

I wish I could see the expression on your face as you read that sentence. You may be saying to yourself, "I could no more give a speech in front of that many people than I could get myself elected president! I'd be afraid to talk in front of a class or even a group of fifteen people. Don't try to tell me I could talk in front of 300!"

Before you jump to that conclusion, let's look at this situation a little more closely. I'm sure you can talk interestingly and convincingly to just one other person—your closest friend perhaps—about some subject that really interests you. The subject doesn't particularly matter: it could be sports, your children, or a special hobby. But whatever it is, you can be interesting and convincing about this subject to one other person.

If you can do this with one person, there is no theoretical reason why you couldn't add 299 other people and talk interestingly and convincingly to an audience of 300. Except for your Repressor. For your Repressor will be saying to you: "Look at all those people out there! You might fail and make a fool of yourself. You've never done anything like this before. Better not even try it—that way you won't have a failure chalked up against you."

And only by conquering the fears prompted by your Repressive Self can you ever prove that you do have the ability to give that speech!

I want to make it clear that I am not promising any "instant miracles" in this book. If you were badly overweight, and a new diet book promised you could slim down in a week, you would be properly skeptical. Similarly, you would be skeptical if I promised that you could discover and use your psychological potentialities overnight.

What I do promise you is that with a careful reading of this book you can discover the aspects of your Repressive Self that are keeping you from being that creative and self-confident little toddler you once were and keeping you from being the unique and creative adult you could become *right now*. I will give you specific tasks to accomplish which will enable you to change your life, *one step at a time*, so that you can gradually free your Potential Self. When we talk about personality fulfillment, do not expect instant miracles. But you will be amazed at what can be accomplished in discovering and actualizing your Potential, if you will follow the patient, one-step-at-a-time approach outlined in this book.

In the next chapter I'm going to help you identify your particular type of Repressive Self. Identification of the problem is the first giant step toward solving it. I will try to help you make this step the beginning in setting free the creative and self-confident toddler within you, who has been trying to cast off his chains for so many years.

2. Your Repressive Self

As I have said, when you were born you had tremendous capacities for creativity and love within you: your Potential Self. You were fortunate if you had truly loving parents who were able to accept your particular uniqueness. If you grew up unhindered by parental pressures, then you gradually developed your potentialities for creativity and for love.

Unfortunately, many people were not raised this way. And that may be true of you. It is possible your parents were not so loving and warm and giving, particularly since our society does not train parents to understand children and accept their unique qualities *as children*. So instead of encouraging you to become the unique person you are, your parents may have made you an inadequate carbon copy of the person *they* wanted you to be. Because of emotional difficulties and unresolved problems stemming from *their* own childhoods, your parents may have instilled in you fears and resentments. Rather than encourage you to develop self-confidence, they may have subtly disparaged and undermined you. Perhaps they dominated you. Or unconsciously attempted to use you to fulfill their own frustrated ambitions.

Your parents did not have to be overtly cruel or domineering. They may have prevented you from developing your Potential Self in very subtle ways. And they may have been firmly convinced that they were doing this all for your own good. They may have, in one way or another, distorted and stifled your personality, so that today you are only a third of the person you might have become. In other words, your parents could have developed in you as a child what psychologists call "anxiety."

Please do not confuse *anxiety* with *fear*. When I use the word *fear*, I am speaking of a realistic emotion which you feel when confronted with a dangerous situation. If two burly men accost you late at night intending to hold you up and mug you, you will feel fear. It would be abnormal if you did not. Fear is an appropriate response to a situation which is realistically dangerous.

Anxiety is quite different. Anxiety is not a response to outside danger, but a response to *inside* danger. When you were a growing child, your parents probably taught you to be afraid of displeasing them. What "displeasing your parents" means will vary enormously from child to child. It may mean not being successful in school. It may mean expressing angry feelings. It may mean expressing sexual feelings. It may mean not having other children who like you. It may mean departing from the image of the "good, obedient, respectful child."

In all probability you, like many children, grew up with a set of invisible parents within your head. You were quite aware of what these invisible parents would think of your actions and feelings. And if they disapprove of your actions or feelings, you experience this devastating emotion we call *anxiety*. Anxiety comes in all sizes, from the smallest size, a momentary feeling of uneasiness, to the largest size, a full-scale attack of panic. People with "anxiety attacks" do not know why they feel nervous and panicky at times. Actually, they are afraid of displeasing the invisible parents in their head, but that is below the level of their conscious awareness. They might experience these anxiety attacks in a church, a theater, or while driving, and have an overwhelming impulse to get out of that situation, but they could not consciously tell you what they were afraid of.

We will do almost anything to ward off this uncomfortable emotion of anxiety. And one of the principal ways we unconsciously choose is to develop a Repressive Self as a protection. The Repressive Self, in other words, is your particular system of psychological defenses which you use to ward off the crippling emotion of anxiety.

There are three main types of Repressive Self. Here I am greatly indebted to the late Dr. Karen Horney, for her very accurate description of these types. She points out that there are three basic ways in which we can express our relationships to other people: we can move *toward* them, *against* them, or *away* from them.

All of these ways of relating to people are healthy if used in moderation and in their right place. There are times when we need to move *toward* people, in love, friendship, and affection. There are times when we need to move *against* people, to assert ourselves, to say "no," and to stand up for our own rights. There are times when we need to move *away from* other people, to reestablish our own inner equilibrium.

So I'm not speaking of normal aspects of moving toward, against, or away from others, but rather of the exaggerated and neurotic forms of relating to people. These neurotic forms of relating to others are three main types of Repressor, which I call the *appeaser*, the *aggressor*, and the *retreater*.

Before I begin to describe these three types of Repressive Self, let me make it clear that no one is one type, pure and simple. Most of us are mixtures of the three. Generally, however, one type will predominate, and we will be mainly appeasers or aggressors or retreaters in our relationships with other people.

Let's begin by describing the *appeaser*.

If your Repressive Self happens to take this form, as a child you were a good little boy or girl. Whenever you and your parents were on the outs, your typical way of trying to put things right was to move *toward* them, to be overdependent on them, and to appease.

If you felt somewhat angry with them, these feelings made you uncomfortable and anxious. You could sense that being angry would displease the silent parents inside. You quickly learned to stifle your own angry and assertive feelings. You assured yourself, "I don't like to fight." Desperately you tried to get your parents to love you as a way of protecting yourself against anxiety. In other words, yours was a tremendous need for affection and approval. And you protected yourself against anxiety by overdependency upon others.

Your exaggerated needs, therefore, are to be liked, wanted, appreciated, taken care of, and guided. At this point you may ask, "But isn't it normal to want other people to like you?" Yes it is, *up to a point*. But you want *everyone* to like you, all the time. And human relations just don't work that way.

You try to avoid quarrels or competition or disagreements at all costs. As a child you always tried to live up to the expectations of others. With your parents, schoolmates, and later with all other people, you tended to subordinate yourself, to take second place to everybody else.

Your pattern is to blame yourself rather than others when things go wrong. It is quite typical of the appeaser who is a blame-acceptor to marry a spouse who is a blame-giver. It is generally hard for you to assert yourself, be critical, give orders, or strive for ambitious goals.

You assume that other people are superior to you, and you probably suffer from a general sense of inadequacy and inferiority. You tend to worry about what others think. You particularly worry if you feel that other people dislike you, or are irritated at you. Any word of criticism is taken as a great rejection.

In other words, you rate yourself by what others think of you. Your self-esteem rises or falls with their approval or disapproval. You tend to be a chameleon, adapting your coloration to what others expect of you rather than having the courage to be your own unique set of personality colors. Your unconscious motto is: *"Everyone must like me at all times, or I am lost. Someone must help me, because I am too weak and powerless to manage by myself."*

You are hypersensitive to anything that remotely smacks of rejection. You may apply things that are said by others to you personally. (Like the husband who commented to his wife, "The trouble with women is that they always take things personally." At which his wife bristled and said, "Well, I certainly don't!") You probably can't take teasing very well, for to you this means criticism and rejection.

If you are married, chances are you have a great deal of trouble standing up to your spouse. You go along with things "so as not to rock the boat" and then hate yourself for it afterwards. In a quarrel, you almost always initiate the first move to make up, because it is intolerable for you to be on the outs with someone.

If you are a parent, you may have difficulty in disciplining your children. Basically you are afraid to take your children to task if they need it, for fear of losing their love. You can't say "no" to them and mean it. You cover up this unpleasant truth by telling yourself: "Well, I'm certainly not going to bring up my children in the authoritarian, dictatorial way my parents raised me!"

The basic problem with you as the appeaser is that you have submerged a whole side of your personality: the side which enables you to be aggressive or hostile if the occasion demands it, or to stand up for your rights when you need to. And you cannot possibly actualize your Potential Self as long as your capacity for *normal aggression* remains repressed. You are like an army which is expected to win a war without guns or ammunition.

This particular type of Repressive Self is the most socially acceptable of the three types. In fact, if you are an appeaser, you are probably well-liked by others, simply because you try so hard to be agreeable. You let yourself be imposed upon, and when other people discover this, they may tend to use you. But they will love you for being a door-mat! In fact, sometimes other people tell you: "You are absolutely the nicest person I know!"

The catch is, of course, that your whole way of life is not built upon the solid rock of your Potential Self but on the shaky neurotic foundation of your Repressive Self. For it is really not very satisfactory to live as you do. Deep down you hate yourself for not being more aggressive and not standing up for yourself. You would *like* to have more self-confidence and drive. When other people impose, it secretly rankles you. Deep within you there is an emotional hunger to be released from the prison of your Repressor and to discover your Potential, which is capable, assertive, and active.

Let's move on to the second main type of Repressive Self: the *aggressor*.

You relate to other people by moving *against* them. Your reaction to your parents was not to be a good little boy or girl and put yourself out to please them, but to fight back. You rebelled against them, sometimes openly, sometimes behind their backs.

As a youngster perhaps you had severe temper tantrums. As an adolescent you probably rebelled against all that your parents stood for. When they tried to control you or mold you to their wishes, instead of giving in and trying to win them over, you fought back.

Your unconscious motto is: *Life is a struggle that someone has to win—and it better be me!* Your primary needs are for power and prestige. You want control over other people and you want success. These are your main goals in life. You feel strong only when achieving a notable success, when others have acclaimed you, or when you have obtained a position of power. To you, it isn't so much how you play the game; it's whether you win or lose. And the name of the game is success.

As a youngster you probably were quite ruthless in the way you pushed other kids around and got your own way. But, of course, as you grew older, you learned that you had to become more subtle. You learned not to let people realize that you manipulate them to do things your way. Often your basically dog-eat-dog attitude toward life is covered over with a smooth front of good fellowship. You learn how to get ahead of a competitor very smoothly. You mask your naked aggressive power ploys.

Of course, all of this is on an unconscious level. You would be highly indignant if anyone accused you of trying to dominate others or push them around!

Your attitude toward your work may be quite revealing. You give the impression of utter fascination and absorbing interest in your work. But it may be very hard for you to relax. You suffer from what psychology calls "Sunday neurosis." That is, when Sundays and vacation times roll around, you don't know what to do with yourself. Often you will find reasons why it's necessary to spend much of your so-called spare time working on something, rather than enjoying yourself. You may complain about how little time you have for your hobbies, or how long it's been since you've had a *real* vacation. However, when you finally do manage to take time off for a family vacation, it may take most of the vacation just to unwind and settle down to begin to enjoy yourself.

Your wife's most typical complaint is that she doesn't see enough of you, and that you spend too little time with the children; and that even when you are there physically, you are still mentally preoccupied with your work.

In spite of the fact that you work hard and compulsively, if we dig beneath the surface, we see that basically you get little genuine joy and pleasure from your work. And sometimes you wish you could chuck it all.

Dominated by the twin goals of success and

power, you have a deep underlying fear of failure. Even when you succeed at one job and one goal, you rarely enjoy it, because you are already looking for bigger and better successes. Your own previous success may be a hard act to follow. And there's the added fear that you may fail in your next undertaking. In later life, when you have advanced as far as possible, you may begin to feel a vague sort of restlessness. It's as if you were not quite satisfied with life, but don't know exactly what is the matter.

In contrast to the appeaser, who hates arguments and quarrels, you thrive on them. You love to play the role of the devil's advocate. You enjoy games of competition where you can pit your strength and skill against others. Of course, you don't particularly enjoy any game if you find that you lose consistently!

In marriage you have little trouble in standing up to your partner. Usually you marry the appeaser type anyway, because your unconscious radar has told you that this is the kind of person you can dominate.

Whereas the appeaser is afraid to say no to his or her children, you have no trouble laying down the law. Unconsciously you take a lot of your need to dominate people out on your children (as well as your spouse)!

Of course, you try to dominate your friends too, even though you may not be aware of it. You want to be right all the time. You are irritated if proved wrong, even in small details. You want your own way and dislike others who don't do what you expect. You are often impatient of any delay, such as a traffic tie-up or a line at the supermarket.

Your way of life, however, is really no more satisfactory than that of the appeaser. Outwardly you may be successful and in a position of leadership, but inwardly you also feel frustrated and dissatisfied with yourself. With that constant threat of failure hanging over you, you need to succeed at *everything* you attempt.

The most basic fact about you is that your psychological center of gravity is outside yourself. The appeaser's center of gravity is outside himself too, because his self-esteem rises or falls according to whether or not other people like him. Since what is important to you is to be successful and powerful, that also places your psychological center of gravity outside yourself. Your internal self-esteem depends on outward success and power. Should you experience unexpected failure in something, it may actually put you on the verge of panic.

Whereas the appeaser has repressed the aggressive side of his personality, you have repressed the tender, playful, warm, and loving side of yours.

Your twin goals of success and power have impoverished the emotional side of your personality. Reaching out for warmth and affection, for closeness, for touching, for enjoying the simple pleasures of life with people you love—all have been stifled in your life. What a fearful emotional price! You have achieved success and power, but somehow you sense that you have missed the things in life that are really important. More than one wife divorces her husband or seeks an affair because she feels that her husband is really married to his work. More than one father dimly senses, somewhere around the edges of his life, that his children are growing up almost as strangers to him. And he may ask himself in unexpected moments, "Is it *really* worth it all?"

Deep within you, as within the appeaser, there is a great desire to strike off the shackles of your Repressor and to discover your Potential Self. What you basically want out of life, though you may not be fully aware of it, is to love and to be loved. And no matter how successful you are, it will not bring love. Admiration—perhaps. Grudging respect —perhaps. But not love.

Finally, let's talk about the third main type of Repressive Self: the *retreater*.

This name describes well the last type of Repressive Self because your reaction to life is to retreat within yourself, the way a turtle draws into its shell. You relate to people by emotionally moving away from them.

Your reaction to your parents, when they hurt your feelings or were unkind, was not to try to win them over as the appeaser did, or to rebel as the aggressor did. Your reaction was to retreat within yourself for comfort and consolation where they couldn't reach you emotionally. You built an emotional cocoon around yourself where no one could touch you. There you felt safe. Emotionally you moved away—first from your parents, then your schoolmates, and finally from people in general.

This reaction probably began far back in your childhood, so far back, in fact, that perhaps you cannot remember it. When you were a toddler playing with blocks, for example, your block tower may have fallen down and other children laughed. You didn't try to build the tower again. Already, at that young age, you were beginning to feel: "It's best not to try anything new!" Because if you didn't try new things, at least other people wouldn't laugh at you or hurt your feelings if you failed.

So you drew into your shell. As a child you stood on the sidelines and watched other children play rather than join in the game. As an adolescent you preferred the solitary walk rather than the party, listening to records in your room rather than attending the rock concert. You chose to be a spectator of life.

As a child you may have discovered the world of books or the world of TV and movies. Perhaps you found that these worlds were safer and less threatening than the world of people. Books or TV would not criticize you. They never made demands on you. Books or TV could not turn against you or let you down as people would.

Or it may be that as a child you discovered the world of pets. If you were really honest with yourself, you actually loved your pets, your dogs or cats or hamsters, better than people. Your pets were always loyal. You could count on them to love you, whereas people were quite unpredictable. And pets were never cruel to you the way other children sometimes were.

Your unconscious motto is: *People have the power to hurt you, if you let yourself get emotionally involved, if you let them get too close to you. So the best thing to do is to retreat. Keep your emotional distance and keep to yourself.*

Your two great neurotic needs are for self-sufficiency and for privacy. Of course, everyone needs a certain amount of self-sufficiency and privacy, but you carry it to extraordinary lengths. You are very closemouthed. You resent questions about your personal life. You walk very gingerly in the whole area of relationships with other people. You don't give much of yourself in your relationships. Even after fifteen years of marriage your wife or husband may say, "I still don't really know what kind of person I married."

You are hypersensitive to anything resembling coercion. That's why it's hard for you to make long-term commitments to anything or anybody. You don't like to feel obligated to anyone. You don't like to be too involved.

Marriage probably represented an unconscious threat to you. You may have had several broken engagements. Finally when you did decide to get married, there may have been a sudden onset of panicky feelings just before the wedding. You wondered to yourself—"What in the world am I doing here? Maybe I'm crazy to take such a big, demanding step like this!"

You can function much better in the more impersonal atmosphere of the business world than the close intimate relationship which a marriage forces upon you. In a marriage relationship there is a demand for you to give up your exaggerated needs for self-sufficiency and privacy, and to open yourself up to the heart and mind of another person. In short, you must dare to become emotionally vulnerable. But this is the thing you fear the most. You are afraid the other person will hurt you as your parents did.

The unspoken question of the appeaser, whenever he meets a person for the first time, is: "Will he like me?" The unspoken question of the aggressor is: "How strong a competitor is he? Will he be more successful than I am?" Your unspoken question to a stranger is: "Will he interfere with me, or will he leave me alone?" For this is what you want most out of life: the freedom to be left alone. You want to live your life in your own way. Your usual reaction is: "I let other people alone and don't bother them. Why don't they let me alone?"

The goals of the appeaser and aggressor are positive. The appeaser wants everybody to like him. The aggressor wants to become successful and powerful. But your goals are basically negative. Your goals are *not* to need anyone, *not* to try new things.

You are afraid of new situations, afraid to venture out where you might be ridiculed for failure. Whereas the aggressor loves to be in the limelight —to be chairperson of a committee, to be in front of people—this is most distasteful to you. If you belong to an organization, you prefer behind-the-scenes work. The worst thing you can imagine is to have to get up in front of people and give a speech.

You prefer to move in well established and comfortable routines. Other people might call them ruts. But they make you feel secure within yourself. Long ago you learned that if you don't try anything new, no one can laugh, hurt, or ridicule you.

Perhaps I should point out that in certain respects everyone is part "retreater." All of us retreat from some new things. You may be quite at home in the world of popular music but "retreat" from classical music because it is strange and you know little about it. Or you may be at ease with things like gardening, stamp collecting, or hi-fi, but you are a retreater when it comes to sports or camping. You may be afraid to try to learn to swim or skate or play tennis or golf.

If your main approach to life is to retreat from it, you are as unsatisfied as the appeaser or the aggressor. The appeaser, by constantly trying to ingratiate himself with people, does not get genuine love from others. And he lacks self-respect because of his inability to assert himself. The aggressor, striving so frantically for success and power, does not find love by his life style either. And neither do you with your unconscious strategy of trying to keep your emotional distance from people.

True, emotional distance can protect you from being hurt. But at the same time it also prevents you from being truly and deeply loved. And that, after all, is what you want deep down inside. Your basic human needs are not different from others. And the most basic human need is to be loved and to love in return. Until this basic need is met, you will never find real and lasting happiness.

Now that you have finished reading these descriptions of the three main types of Repressive Self, I want to warn you about something. You may have a tendency to be upset, to feel somewhat depressed or guilty as you recognize yourself in one or more of the three types. You may be feeling right now: "Gosh, that really describes me. It's almost as if you knew me personally. I always figured I wasn't worth much, and now I know it, when I see myself described in such detail!"

If you do feel this way, remember that I did not write these descriptions for the purpose of making you feel guilty or worthless. As a matter of fact, it is likely your Repressor is at work again, using these descriptions as a means to torture you, to make you feel bad about yourself.

Remember that what I am describing is your *Repressive Self*, not your *Potential Self*. And the whole purpose of this book is to help you, a step at a time, to get rid of your Repressive Self in order to develop your unique and Potential Self.

Chances are you have misdirected much of the emotional energy of your life. The energy and effort which should have gone into the development of your Potential Self, which is capable of loving and being loved and of productive and creative work, has gone instead into the development of your Repressive Self, which neurotically seeks to appease people, to compete with them for success and power, or to emotionally retreat from them.

These three main types of Repressor stand in your way as you strive to become your Potential Self. Furthermore, your Repressor uses a number of psychological defense mechanisms, which consume your time and energy and prevent you from becoming your Potential Self. We will talk about these defense mechanisms in our next chapter.

3: The Defense Mechanisms That Imprison You

In the previous chapter I discussed the difference between anxiety and fear. Fear is an appropriate response to an outside danger. Anxiety, a normal response to an inside danger, may be appropriate in childhood but is inappropriate in adulthood. It is the intolerable emotion a child feels when he is afraid he has displeased his parents. Later, anxiety becomes the intolerable emotion that the child, now grown to an adult, feels when he is afraid he may displease the invisible parents in his head.

In the previous chapter we also talked about the three main types of Repressive Self, the three ways in which people try to ward off anxiety. To

50

the extent that a person devotes his energies to one of the three types of Repressor, he cannot develop his Potential Self.

Therefore, a person who spends his life appeasing other people, or frantically searching for success and power, or retreating from emotional involvement with others is preventing himself from developing his dormant Potential Self.

Unfortunately, the hampering influence of the Repressive Self is not limited to the three main types. The Repressor uses a number of psychological defense mechanisms which also prevent you from becoming aware of what you really think and feel.

"Defense mechanism" is a term which many people use but few understand. For an illustration of how few people understand this term, the next time you hear it used, ask naively, "You know there's something I've always wondered about. What does a defense mechanism defend you against?" The person will probably be unable to answer. So I'm going to.

The purpose of a defense mechanism is to protect you, not against other people as many believe, but *against feelings within yourself*. It is created by your mind to handle that devastating emotion of anxiety which occurs when you think or do something that would displease the invisible parents in your mind. And what is the main thing that would displease them? Having certain feelings within yourself, mainly hostile feelings or sexual feelings, perhaps feelings of inadequacy or inferiority, sometimes even feelings of love or warmth. Therefore, the purpose of the defense mechanism is to keep you completely unaware that you are feeling angry or sexy or hurt or inadequate.

Since defense mechanisms operate on an unconscious level, the individual is completely unaware that he feels certain emotions within himself, because the defense mechanism blocks out the emotions.

It is difficult then, to say the least, for you to deal realistically with a situation when you are totally unaware of your feelings. This will become clearer as I describe the defense mechanisms and give examples of how they work.

REPRESSION

Repression means that thoughts or feelings are pushed down into the unconscious mind, and an individual is totally unaware of them. That this can happen has been proved through thousands of psychological experiments, particularly those involving the use of hypnosis. However, I prefer to illustrate this with a startling but clear-cut example from clinical practice. Many years ago I worked as a psychologist in a mental hospital. Following a staff conference and a thorough psychological evaluation of a particular patient, we brought him into the room to be interviewed.

The psychiatrist in charge of the case was very gentle in interviewing him. At one point he mentioned that during the previous weekend the patient's wife had come to visit him. The psychiatrist said, "The staff noticed you seemed irritated at your wife's visit." The patient snapped back, "I was not at all irritated!" The psychiatrist followed this with, "You seem a little irritated when I question you about this." The patient responded, "You are wrong, sir, dead wrong! I am not irritated at all; you may question me about anything you please!" The psychiatrist tried again, "Excuse me for mentioning it again, sir, but it seems that you are more than irritated; you are somewhat angry when we discuss the subject of your wife." At this, the patient pounded the table with his fist and said in a furious tone of voice, "I am not in the slightest bit angry, and, in fact, I have never been angry at anyone in my whole life!"

To those in the room it was obvious that here was a man who was furiously angry unconsciously, but on the conscious level he was totally unaware that he was experiencing such feelings. And his remark that he had never been angry at anyone in his whole life was a tip-off: he had probably been taught by his parents that it was a very bad thing to do. Naturally this man was at a great disadvantage in handling his relationship with his wife and the angry feelings he had about her. His defense mechanism of repression had pushed these feelings into his unconscious mind, where he was totally unaware of his anger.

Psychological slips of the tongue often betray the existence of repressed feelings. In these "Freudian" slips, our conscious mind means to say one thing, but our unconscious knows our true feelings. Sometimes we end up saying something completely unexpected and frequently funny.

·I recall one young married woman I was counseling. She claimed that her parents had brought her up in a normal healthy manner with regard to sex and that all she needed was some information on sexual techniques in marriage. I lent her a book called *Sex Without Guilt*. During her appointment the next week she handed me the book back and said, "Oh, Dr. Dodson, this was really helpful. Thank you so much for lending me the book *Guilt Without Sex*." She was totally unaware of her slip of the tongue until I brought it to her attention. After she understood its meaning, we could explore how she had fooled herself that her parents were open and straightforward about sex. Actually they had filled her with guilt feelings. Although her true feelings about sex were repressed, her slip of the tongue showed they were down there in her unconscious mind.

Repression is being discussed as the first defense mechanism because it is involved in all of the other defense mechanisms. Repression is the pushing of thoughts and feelings down into the unconscious, and *all* defense mechanisms do that. Technically we should say "projection and repression" or "intellectualization and repression," but it isn't necessary if you just take it for granted that repression is a part of every other defense mechanism.

I also want to clarify the difference between repression and suppression. People often use the two words interchangeably, which is unfortunate. They do not mean the same thing. Repression means that thoughts or feelings are pushed down into your unconscious mind and you are totally unaware of them. Suppression means that you are quite aware of certain feelings, but you choose not to bring them out. For example, with a *repressed* feeling of anger toward your boss, you are unaware that you feel angry toward him. With a *suppressed* feeling of anger, you will be quite aware of how you feel, but you will not express these feelings to him because it would not be in your best interest. Surely you can see that if you have repressed feelings of anger and rage toward your boss, you are going to be handicapped in your dealings with him. For only when we are aware of all of the feelings we have toward the important people in our lives can we do a good job of handling these relationships.

DENIAL OF REALITY

This mechanism is the simplest, the most primitive, and usually the first that a young child uses. In fact, with very young children, it is difficult to know when it is conscious and when it is unconscious. The mechanism is simplicity itself: whatever is disagreeable or unpleasant is simply blotted out of the mind, as if the mind is saying: "I don't want that to be true, so it isn't true."

A hilarious example of this occurred when my oldest boy was a little over two. We were going to the park one Saturday afternoon and I told him to get his coat.

"I don't need it."

"Yes you do, Randy, it's cold out."

"I don't know where it is."

"Well, let's go back to your bedroom and see if it's hanging on its hook."

We went to his room, and sure enough, there was the coat, hanging right where it was supposed to be.

Randy stood right in front of it and said, "I'm not going to see it!"

Of course, with adults denial of reality does not work in quite such obvious ways. But I recall a twenty-eight-year-old woman I saw in therapy, whose boy friend was killed in an airplane crash. Her main way of handling this was by a massive denial of reality. For several months she came in with the same feelings: "I can't believe he's dead. My mind tells me it did happen, but my feelings say no, it couldn't have happened, and he'll come walking in the door tonight just like he used to."

This woman represents an extreme example of the ways in which many adults use denial of reality. They may refuse to discuss "unpleasant things." In effect, they are refusing to face the difficult or unpleasant problems that need to be dealt with. Have you ever had the experience of confronting someone with some needed criticism and thought you had finally gotten your point across to him? Then he makes a remark that astounds you, because he could not possibly say such a thing if what you said *really* registered. The answer, of course, is that what you said did *not* truly register. He blotted it out and denied the unpleasant psychological realities you were trying to communicate.

Once again, you can see how such a defense mechanism hampers us. Reality is reality and it doesn't change just because we deny it. All we do is handicap ourselves by not facing it.

I remember a college student with whom I did vocational counseling. He wanted to become a doctor. He showed a definite interest in medicine and medical research. Unfortunately, his IQ was nowhere near the level that would be required for him to get into medical school, much less to graduate. As gently as possible, I explained this to him. I suggested that his best bet would be to become a medical technician. He heard me but would have none of it. "Intelligence tests don't tell everything; I *know* I can make it as a doctor!" Well, he could deny reality all he wanted, but it was still there. He was turned down by every single medical school he applied to. He did finally become a medical technician, but only after going through the totally unnecessary trauma of being rejected by medical schools, due to his own denial of reality.

NEGATION

This is a sophisticated adult version of denial of

reality. Sigmund Freud, many years ago, first discovered the existence of negation. He noticed that patients would say things such as "Dr. Freud, I have a lot of problems I need your help with, but I want you to know I have no problems with my father." Freud would say to himself, "Hmmm—I wonder why he goes out of his way to tell me he has no problems with his father? Must have a lot of problems there!"

This is how negation works. A person states how he does *not* think or feel about something, which means that is exactly how he *does* think or feel in his unconscious mind. (Note that the person must make this statement "out of the blue"; if he makes the statement in answering a question it does not count as a negation.)

Here are some commonplace examples of negations. A person says, "Not to change the subject, but . . ." And what happens next? He changes the subject! Or someone will say, "I don't want to start an argument, but . . ." And then he says something that is sure to start an argument. Or a person will say, "Now I don't mean this to put you down," and then he says something that most decidedly does put you down.

Politicians' utterances are often full of negations. One politician who had just lost the election for governor of California, said in his concession speech,

"I want you to know I bear in my heart *no malice* toward my worthy opponent, and especially I harbor *no ill will* toward the voters of the great state of California who elected him."

Knowing how negation works will not only help you to become aware of your real feelings about some things, but it can also help you discover the true attitudes of others. I heard a delightful story about negation from one of my patients. He came in one day and told me this anecdote about his twelve-year-old son. The boy had been teased and tormented by a bigger boy in his class. Finally he decided to do something about it. He confronted the bigger boy and said, "Look, you'd better knock it off or you and I are going to have a fight." The bigger boy replied, "Fight a little runt like you? Don't make me laugh! Of course it's not that I'm afraid to fight you or anything like that." My patient's son said, "As soon as he said that stuff about not being afraid to fight, I recognized it was a negation, Dad, and I popped him one, and he ran!"

From teaching defense mechanisms to both high school and college students, I have found that it is often upsetting for people to learn about this particular one. The reason is that they hear themselves and others using it so often. It is upsetting to realize that they are hiding feelings and thoughts they are not aware of. This may happen to you too. If it does, I hope you will try to take a long-range view. It is far better for you to become aware of your true unconscious thoughts and feelings than to fool yourself and be handicapped in dealing with reality.

DISPLACEMENT

In this defense mechanism, feelings actually directed toward one person or situation are displaced or shifted toward another person or situation. A classic example of this is a cartoon showing the boss giving his employee a bawling out. The employee goes home, and as soon as he gets in the door he yells at his wife for some trifle. The wife, in turn, scolds her child, and the child kicks the dog! Each one is afraid to confront and deal with the person with whom he is really angry, so he displaces it to someone else.

Another typical way displacement works is to displace feelings from important areas of life to trivial things. Classical examples include bitter marital quarrels over who left the cap off the toothpaste tube or whether the bacon was too done. Here the couple are obviously afraid to face and resolve the important psychological conflicts between them, so they displace their feelings of hostility to petty and trivial differences.

Clearly, displacement makes it impossible for a person to deal with the real situations that are bothering him and find constructive solutions to his interpersonal difficulties. Displacement says to him: "Don't look here (at the real problem); look over there (at this phony issue)."

REACTION FORMATION

This is a poor title, because it does not describe the defense mechanism very clearly, but we are stuck with it in the psychological literature, so I might as well use it. Reaction formation means the formation of a reaction on the conscious level, which is the exact opposite of what is going on at an unconscious level.

The key to reaction formation is the excessive and rigid character of the attitudes expressed. A person who is truly loving will show this by attitudes of love, care, and respect for other individuals. But a person who is continually overwhelming you with sweet talk and telling you constantly how much he or she loves you . . . such a person is probably a victim of reaction formation. Underneath their cloying sweetness, these persons probably harbor intense feelings of anger and hostility, which are totally unknown to them and totally unacceptable to their conscious picture of themselves.

The time to suspect reaction formation is when

you find an individual whose conscious attitudes on a particular subject are superstrong and rigid. Underneath, his unconscious mind has the exact opposite feelings. A few years ago a prominent minister in San Francisco was well-known for his denunciation of vice, particularly prostitution. Other ministers had similar attitudes, but they did not make it a life and death issue. One day he was found in a hotel room with a prostitute, and naturally the story hit the front pages of every newspaper in the city. What had been happening? At an unconscious level he was powerfully tempted by prostitution. Yet he was saying to himself unconsciously, "If I crusade powerfully against vice and prostitution, then I can prove to myself and others that these things hold no attraction for me." Unfortunately, his defense mechanism did not work successfully, and he finally succumbed to the very urges he had been trying to fight against for so long. Once again, you can see how defense mechanisms get in the way of our effective functioning.

Had the minister been able to admit to himself that he actually had urges to seek out the services of a prostitute, he could have consulted a therapist and worked out a solution to this problem.

Fanatics of any sort (religious, political, or otherwise) are good examples of reaction formation. Their fanatical and excessive zeal for their cause betrays the fact that they unconsciously doubt the beliefs that consciously they hold so dear.

One of the things that often happens to people using reaction formation is that the feelings they are unconsciously covering up "leak out." If you are observant you can catch glimpses of their true feelings. Here is a classic example.

Antivivisectionists are people who are emotional over the fact that scientists use animals in research work. They claim that the scientists are cruel and sadistic in their animal research. By contrast, the antivivisectionist paints himself as a kind and caring person who loves all living things. Dr. Jules Masserman, a psychiatrist, who used cats in his research on alcoholism, received the following letter from an antivivisectionist. One does not have to dig very deeply to see the unconscious attitudes of hostility and sadism which this "kindhearted person" is covering up by his reaction formation of antivivisectionism:

> . . . I read (a magazine article) . . . on your work on alcoholism . . . I am surprised that anyone who is as well educated as you must be to hold the position that you do would stoop to such depths as to torture helpless little cats in the pursuit of a cure for alcoholics . . . A drunkard does not want to be cured— a drunkard is just a weak-minded idiot who belongs

in the gutter and should be left there. Instead of torturing helpless little cats why not torture the drunks, or better still exert your would-be noble effort toward getting a bill passed to *exterminate* the drunks. They are not any good to anyone or themselves and are just a drain on the public, having to pull them off the street, jail them, then they have to be fed while there and its against the law to feed them arsenic so there they are . . . if people are such weaklings the world is better off without them.

. . . My greatest wish is that you have brought home to you a torture that will be a thousand fold greater than what you have and are doing to the little animals . . . If you are an example of what a noted psychiatrist should be I'm glad I am just an ordinary human being without a letter after my name. I'd rather be just myself with a clear conscience, *knowing I have not hurt any living creature* and can sleep without seeing frightened, terrified dying cats—because I know they must die after you have finished with them. No punishment is too great for you and I hope I live to read about your mangled body and long suffering before you finally die—and I'll laugh long and loud.[1]

1. Masserman, J. H.: *Principles of Dynamic Psychiatry*, 2nd ed. (Philadelphia: W. B. Saunders Company, 1961), p. 38.

As you can see, the person who uses reaction formation as a defense often has his whole life organized around a series of exaggerated and rigid beliefs, which make it very difficult to deal openly and flexibly with other people. He cannot solve his own problems as long as his defenses get in the way.

PROJECTION

In the defense mechanism of projection a person takes his own feelings and projects them outward onto someone else. The following is an extreme example of this. A sweet little grandmotherly type consulted me for help. At first she hemmed and hawed, and finally asked if she could speak perfectly frankly. I assured her that everything we talked about was completely confidential. "Well," she said, "the problem is that my landlady is trying to poison the water supply in my apartment, and I don't know what to do about it." Closer questioning revealed that she had moved to this particular apartment house because she believed her previous landlady had been seeping poison gas under her door.

As we delved further into the subject, it became clear that both landladies had done various things which had irritated and angered her. But she had not been consciously aware of this, for she had been taught as a child that being angry was bad. Since she could not admit to being angry at these landladies, she could not work out the problems between her and them in a realistic manner. Her use of projection was so extreme that it became a delusion of persecution. The defense mechanism took this form: "I'm not angry at my landlady, because nice women never get angry. No, she is angry at me. In fact, she's trying to poison my water supply and kill me."

A less extreme example of projection can be seen in another clinical case. A nineteen-year-old girl in the course of a therapy session confessed that she and her boy friend had indulged in oral sex the past week. After she finished relating this, she said, "I can tell by the look on your face that you're thoroughly disgusted with me, and you probably don't want me to come here anymore. . . ." I pointed out to her that I had no such feelings and that it was she who was condemning herself so harshly and then projecting that condemnation onto me.

If more parents were aware of the widespread use of projection, they would have a key to understanding the many puzzling fears of their children. It has been my experience that most parents tend to believe that a child's fears are caused by something frightening that happens *outside* the child. It comes as a great surprise to most parents to learn that it is something *inside* the child which causes the fear. This widespread misunderstanding on the part of parents is unfortunately aided and abetted by magazine articles warning against letting children see "frightening" movies on TV or at a theater, because seeing these movies will allegedly cause the child to develop fears. For the most part this is not true.

The great majority of children's fears are developed through the use of projection. The child is taught to be afraid of his own angry feelings and to feel guilty if he feels anger. I recall vividly one incident in a park where I saw this kind of parental teaching going on. A little boy about four was feeling angry at his little sister and I overheard him saying "I hate you, Peggy!" His mother was horrified at this and immediately said, "Robert! Don't say that! You don't hate Peggy. She's your sweet little sister and you love her!" When a child is taught this kind of thing, he comes to feel: "I'd better not feel angry about anything, because my mother and father will be very displeased if I feel that way!"

After a long enough period of teaching by his

parents, the child becomes afraid to express or even feel his hostile or angry feelings. But since he is human, and feeling angry from time to time is part of being human, what does he do when he feels angry at mother or daddy, brothers or sisters, or friends? The answer is that he often projects the angry feelings on something real or imaginary outside of him. He may have dreams in which he projects his own angry feelings onto wild animals or monsters and flees from these hostile beings in his dream. Or he may have daydreams or scary fantasies in which he is afraid he will be kidnapped, or a burglar will break into the house, or there will be an earthquake in which he will be destroyed. When he has any of these scary dreams or fantasies, it is as if he is saying: "It's not me who's angry or hostile at anybody. No, it's the angry lions or monsters or burglars or earthquakes that are hostile and are trying to hurt or kill me."

This use of projection can be clearly seen in the case of one of my young patients, Karen, a sweet, shy seven-year-old girl. Her parents brought her to me for help because of recurrent nightmares. Almost every night she would have the same nightmare in which she was pursued by some sort of horrible monster. She would awake terrified, and sometimes screaming, from the nightmare. At first her parents thought that perhaps she had seen some frightening movie on TV, and they began to monitor her TV watching very carefully. However, this did nothing to clear up the nightmares, so finally in desperation they brought her to me.

I gave her a thorough battery of psychological tests, plus several talk-and-play sessions in the playroom. The tests revealed that she was a very inhibited and shy child who needed more extensive help than simply eliminating the nightmares. But since the parents were most concerned about the nightmares, I decided to start with that problem.

Once the psychodynamics of her life situation were understood, the reason for the nightmares became clear. It was another example of our old friend projection. Her father teased her all the time. Being a very sensitive child, she just hated it. He would say, in what he thought was simply the spirit of good fun, things like "Karen, your face is so homely you would frighten witches on Halloween." His teasing remarks hurt her deeply and made her very angry, but she kept all these feelings to herself. Instead of being able to let out her angry feelings to her father, she projected them onto the monster of her nightmares.

So I worked with her and gradually arranged for a confrontation between her and her father about how she felt when he teased her. First, I told her father what was happening, and he was shocked to find out her reaction to his teasing. I said she was terribly afraid to tell him her true feelings, and that it would be very hard to get her to do it. But he was cooperative and agreed to encourage her to speak up about her feelings and reassure her she would not be punished for doing so.

Then I worked with her and helped her gain courage and self-confidence so she could tell her father how she felt about the teasing. Finally, I got her to the point where she felt she was ready, and we had a joint session with mother, father, Karen, and me. She was able to tell him how it hurt her feelings and made her mad when he teased her. He told her he was sorry she felt that way. He said he had not meant to hurt her feelings or make her mad, and he promised he would not ever tease her again. We had two more joint family sessions covering the same general ground.

Meanwhile, in separate sessions with Karen I explained to her, on her level of understanding, that instead of being able to tell her father she was mad at him for teasing her, she was projecting these angry feelings onto the monster in her nightmares. I explained that when she would be able to tell her father she was mad, then the angry monster of her dreams would fade away and finally vanish. And that's exactly what happened! As soon as she was able to tell her father she was angry at his teasing, the nightmares began to diminish. In two months, the nightmares were completely gone, and they never came back. A crystal-clear example of what really causes children's fears!

I want to give another example which illustrates, first, what does *not* cause projection in children, and, second, what does. My three children have all been raised to be allowed to speak their feelings freely to their mother and father. If they are angry, they have been allowed and encouraged to express the angry feelings and not keep them bottled up inside. The result is that they have had very little occasion to use the mechanism of projection and have had very few fears.

For example, when my oldest boy, Randy, was ten, he and I went to see the movie *In Cold Blood*. I'm sure this would be very much frowned upon by the writers of some articles in women's magazines, who would "tsk-tsk" severely at the idea of taking a "young, impressionable child" to such a "frightening" movie. Randy had no problem with the movie, and that night he slept as peacefully as a baby. No bad dreams. Obviously the *external* stimulus of a scary movie did not cause fears or bad dreams in Randy.

But then about four months later, Randy and I had a go-around much of the day in which we were quite angry at each other. That night he had a nightmare. Obviously he had not completely released his anger toward me during the day, and it had reappeared via the mechanism of projection in a bad dream that night.

So projection is a very widely used defense mechanism, not only by adults but also by children. Almost all of us use projection more than we realize. Unable to face the existence of certain feelings within ourselves because they conflict with our self-image, we project them onto other people or situations.

RATIONALIZATION

This defense mechanism is probably the closest to the surface. For this reason it is the easiest for most people to realize when it is operating (especially when it is operating in other people!). Rationalization is a mechanism by which you give a plausible or rational explanation for something you have done or something that has happened to you. But the reason you give is not the real one. The schoolboy who fails a test because he didn't study sufficiently, doesn't admit that to himself. Instead he says, "That mean old teacher doesn't like me and doesn't grade fairly."

A medical student told me the following incident in the course of his therapy. One of the black students in his class, named Morris, was bombastic, egocentric, and altogether an obnoxious person. Morris insisted from time to time, "I'm a victim of racial prejudice. You guys don't want to have anything to do with me because I'm black." Finally my medical student, fed up with this, had an eyeball-to-eyeball confrontation with Morris.

"Listen, Morris," he said, "I'm sick and tired of this BS that the guys around here don't like you because you're black. We like the other blacks around here fine. But we don't like you because you're just plain obnoxious. If you learned to act differently, maybe you could make some friends. But first you've got to stop hiding behind all the BS about prejudice."

And that's exactly what Morris was doing. He didn't want to face the fact that his own attitudes and feelings were the real reason the other med students didn't like him. He had to seek another logical and rational-seeming reason. Here again, rationalization, like other defense mechanisms, prevents a person from facing and solving real problems of an interpersonal nature.

FANTASY

This defense mechanism belongs more to childhood and adolescence than to adult life, unless the adult is so severely emotionally disturbed that he is retreating from real life into psychotic fantasy and actually needs to be hospitalized. In fantasy, the individual who is struggling to succeed and reach certain goals in real life, simply turns to fantasy to achieve those goals.

I remember having two fantasy daydreams in my adolescent days. I used them to pass the time in particularly dull classes. In one I was a basketball star who had perfected an unstoppable shot. I could make this shot from underneath my own basket. If the other team ganged up on me to prevent this from happening, I would simply pass off to a teammate who would make the basket and score the winning goal.

In the second fantasy I was the leader of a top-notch band. After every performance girls would cluster around me and beg me to take them out. If you deduce from these two fantasies that I was not achieving the success I wanted with either basketball or girls, you would be right. I was only second team on the basketball squad, and not once do I remember being stampeded by girls begging me for dates. Obviously if I had been a top basketball star, or if I had been an enormous success with the girls, I would never have needed to use these fantasies.

Adults use fantasies also. When husbands discover what they consider deficiencies in their wives, they will often fantasize what it would be like being married to a friend's wife instead. Or if a man encounters problems on his job, he may fantasize solving the problem by taking a new job.

All of us probably have some adult fantasies when reality is not to our liking. It is only when we use the fantasy as a substitute for a realistic confrontation of the problems that the fantasy defense mechanism makes trouble for us.

INTELLECTUALIZATION

In this defense mechanism, emotional reactions that would ordinarily accompany painful events are replaced by intellectual and rational explanations in order to avoid the painful feelings.

Here is a good example of intellectualization. Some time ago I had a patient in group therapy whom others in the group nicknamed "Doctor Freud." He was given this nickname because he avoided discussing his own feelings and instead gave long-winded psychological and intellectual explanations. One time another patient exploded at him. "Harold, you are a miserable excuse for a human being, and I feel like kicking your ass out of this group!"

How did Harold react to this angry outburst? Did he say something like, "Why you lousy son-of-a-bitch, who do you think you are?" Not at all. He intellectualized. "Now Tom, I think I understand why you would say a thing like that. We all know you disliked your father from things you've said. So when you cuss me out, it's obvious that you are projecting your father onto me and that's why you said something like that. Now this problem of yours is something the group can help you with if you'll let us."

In other words, "Dr. Freud" had run true to form. Instead of responding with the feelings that were aroused when the other person attacked him in that fashion, he wove an intellectual verbal co-coon over the whole incident.

People who use this defense mechanism are called intellectualizers. They are people who try to *think* their way through situations which they should *feel* their way through. Basically these people, who are afraid of their feelings, use their intellect instead.

After speaking to an adult group one evening on marriage and family relationships, we held a question and answer period. One man (who turned out to be a scientist) tried earnestly to convince me and the audience that in any case of marital conflict we should use the scientific method to solve it. I tried to persuade him that this was completely inappropriate. I explained that the scientific method was a fine tool for making scientific discoveries and building bridges and airplanes and getting us to the moon. But I pointed out that when it came to resolving conflicts between husband and wife or between parents and children we are in the realm of *feeling*, not in the realm of *thinking*. The scientific method is quite inappropriate here.

My office is situated close to a number of scientific and engineering companies. During the twenty years I have been in clinical practice, therefore, many of the husbands of the marriage counseling cases I have worked with have been scientists or engineers. One of the typical and most basic complaints of the wives has been: "My husband never shows me his feelings. If we have a problem to solve involving the kids, he tries to deal with it as if our child was a broken gauge on a machine instead of a little person with feelings."

People who are uncomfortable in the world of feelings use intellectualization as a defense mechanism. Distrusting and fearing feelings, they turn to the realm of logic, reason, and the intellect, where they feel safe. The parts of life that are amenable to logic, reason, and the intellect they can handle well. But when it comes to those parts of life which do not fit this formula, they flounder badly. Ultimately they find that intellectualizing will not work. Painful as it may be, they must finally turn to their feelings and *feel* their way through the situation.

UNDOING

In this defense mechanism the individual "undoes" or wipes out some thought, impulse, feeling, or action of which the invisible parents in his head would disapprove. Here's how this works. Each individual carries around in his head a little balance scale. Whenever he thinks, feels, or does something which his invisible parents would disapprove of, one side of the scale goes down, and he feels terribly guilty. Now he feels he must put something "good" on the other side of the scale to balance it, to "undo" the bad thought or feeling or action.

In childhood this was relatively simple to accomplish. The child did something he had been taught was wrong (took cookies out of the cookie jar, sassed his mother, masturbated). This sent one side of the balance scale down, and he felt guilty. When his parents found out and spanked him, scolded him, or punished him in some other way, that put something "good" on the other side of the balance scale, and the bad thought or action was "undone."

However, when a child gets to be an adult, things

become much more complicated. The adult may have a "bad" thought, impulse or action on one side of the balance scale, but there are now no parents to punish him and "undo" it. What can he do? His unconscious defense mechanism decides that the only thing to do is to punish himself and that will even the balance scale.

Let me give you an example from adolescence. Many adolescent girls get pregnant due to undoing. The girl has been told by her parents not to engage in sex relations. But she does, and feels terribly guilty. How does her unconscious mind arrange to punish her? Easy—she doesn't use any contraceptives, and the next thing she knows she's pregnant. She has successfully arranged to be punished so that the balance scale can be evened!

Of course, nobody sits down and says, "Let's see how I can punish myself and in that way undo some bad thoughts or feelings." All of the self-punishment is done unconsciously. In more than twenty years of clinical practice, I have seen people unconsciously arrange the most ingenious ways of messing up their jobs, their marriages, and other aspects of their lives. A very good book which describes in detail the self-destructive ways in which people punish themselves is *Man Against Himself* by Dr. Karl Menninger.

Here is an example from my clinical practice of a classical case of undoing.

Wayne, a gruff, stocky man in his early forties, was copartner in a construction business. He had only a high school education, but by sheer drive and ambition he had become a leader and was widely respected in the industry. He and his company were on their way up, but they had not quite "made it big" yet. Then the opportunity they had been looking for came along, a really enormous contract which could boost their company into the big time.

Wayne specialized in doing the bidding for the company, and so he carefully did his figuring and turned in the sealed bid. But that night he woke up from a sound sleep, covered with a cold sweat. The horrible thought came to him that he had bid the job too low.

"This will ruin us!" he thought. "We'll get the job because of my low bid, but we won't be able to make ends meet. Not only will we show no profit, but we'll actually lose a huge amount of dough. If we get the job at that low bid, it will wipe the company out!"

He hurriedly got dressed and drove down to his office in the middle of the night. He refigured the job and ended up with a much higher bid. The next day he retrieved his first sealed bid and substituted the new one.

Two days later, when the bids were opened, another company had gotten the job with a bid just slightly above the first bid Wayne had turned in. Wayne was sick about it, because he realized now that his first bid had been right all along. Had he left it alone, his company would have landed the big contract they had been waiting for so long and would have been able to make a huge profit. Wayne didn't understand how he, an experienced bidder, could have made such a stupid blunder. He was so upset about the whole thing that he came to me for counseling.

"How could I have been so dumb?" he kept saying. "I've been bidding these things for eleven years and I've never made such a stupid mistake before in my life. Here was my chance to put the company over the top and I blew it. Why? Why? Why?"

As I continued seeing Wayne and learned what was going on in his life, the answer to the "why" became clear. He had been carrying on an affair with a secretary in the office for over a year, and he felt very guilty about this. The balance scale in Wayne's mind was tipped way down to one side because of the guilt he felt over the affair. His unconscious mind was telling him he needed to be punished in order to "undo" the guilt feelings. Well, if he made a clever bid on that job, and his company became enormously successful as a result, that could hardly be called punishment. On the other hand, if he messed up the bid, if he goofed things so that his company did not get the job, that would be a just and fitting punishment. The stupid blunder of the bid would "undo" the guilt feelings of the affair.

Of course, Wayne's unconscious handling of the situation by undoing did not deal constructively with either his company's future or his own marital problems.

I pointed out to Wayne that something similar would recur, unless he faced up to the difficulties in his marital situation. I said that the basic reason for the affair was not simply a sexual fling, as he believed on a conscious level, but an unconscious effort to vent his angry feelings toward his wife. I suggested that a much better way of handling the situation was for him to confront his problems directly with his wife and get them out into the open. Wayne finally agreed and somewhat reluctantly decided to give up the affair.

Then I started seeing Wayne and his wife together and working on the unresolved problems between them. It took some solid persistent work on the part of both of them over a period of time, but finally the two were able to establish a new and happier equilibrium in their marriage. And to my knowledge Wayne has not needed to punish himself by making any foolish mistakes in his business since then!

REGRESSION

In this defense mechanism a person "regresses" or goes back to reaction patterns he used when much younger. The classical example of this is when a new baby is born and an older child may go back for awhile to demanding a bottle, sucking the thumb, baby talk, or other infantile reactions. Nurses are familiar with adults who regress in the hospital and become quite childish in their demanding behavior. All of us are vunerable in the face of severe stress and may retreat to more immature patterns of psychological functioning. For most people, regression is kept within bounds and used only occasionally. A severely emotionally ill psychotic person may regress to such a state that he cannot care for himself and needs to be hospitalized.

Well, there they are—eleven different defense mechanisms used by your Repressive Self. The motive behind all of them is the same: to fool yourself so that you're not aware of the certain thoughts and feelings that the invisible parents within your head would disapprove of. If your invisible parents knew you have these thoughts or feelings, you would become terribly anxious. Defense mechanisms protect and defend you against this anxiety by unconsciously blotting thoughts and feelings out of your mind.

But there is a catch to it, as I have been demonstrating throughout the chapter. The catch is that when you are feeling angry or sexy or deeply hurt, *if you do not even know you have these feelings,* you cannot possibly deal with them in a constructive way. The defense mechanisms of your Repressive Self put blinders around you so that you cannot see part of reality. You end up spending an enormous amount of energy in repressing, undoing, intellectualizing or using other defense mechanisms to delude yourself about the feelings going on inside you.

In this chapter I have told you what defense mechanisms are and how they work. In the next chapter you will begin to learn what you can do to break loose from the stranglehold that the Repressive Self and its defense mechanisms have on you.

4. The Power Of Negative Thinking

I think it's time to take stock of where we are in your journey to discover and utilize your Potential Self. Let me summarize what we know so far.

• You were born with an absolutely unique personality, a Potential Self with untapped possibilities for creativity and love. Because of your unique combination of genes, no one else on this planet has ever had your personality, and no one ever will.

• Your Potential Self was fully functioning when you were a young toddler, about one year old. In the same way that you were completely utilizing your Potential at that time, you can learn to actualize your Potential again at your present age.

• When you were a toddler, society (parents, relatives, teachers, etc.) began to curtail and throttle your Potential Self and impose upon you a Repressive Self.

• There are three main types of Repressive Self: the appeaser, the aggressor, and the retreater.

• In addition to belonging to one or more of these types, your Repressor also uses a number of defense mechanisms. The purpose of these is to keep you unaware of feelings you are actually experiencing, but on an unconscious level. For if you were aware of these feelings, you would become very anxious, since you would be displeasing the invisible parents inside your mind.

• Your Repressive Self is the enemy of your Potential Self. Much of the psychological energy that should go into the development of your Potential goes instead into the maintenance of your Repressor and its defense mechanisms.

• So far I have dealt with your Potential Self and your Repressive Self from the viewpoint of diagnosing what is going on. I have done this to help you understand your own potentialities and how your Repressive Self prevents you from using them. But diagnosis is only part of the job. In this sense you are like a patient to whom I have given a battery of psychological tests and then discussed the results with him or her. You know what is causing your psychological problems, but you don't yet know how to solve them.

Now I am going to deal with the practical details of what you can do about solving your problems.

My aim is to teach you two things:

• Specific tactics to break free of your Repressive Self.

• Specific methods to discover and actualize your Potential Self.

The following analogy will give you a clearer understanding of what we are attempting to do. Imagine you are an athlete with the potential of becoming a top-notch swimmer. Unfortunately, an enemy of yours has encased your entire body in a cast from head to foot, and you have no way of developing that aptitude. Then you discover that your one hand is free from the cast and a sharp chipping tool is just within your reach. You now realize that you can chip away your body cast and be free to develop your potential swimming ability. That body cast is your Repressive Self.

So first of all let's talk about the techniques for getting rid of your Repressive Self. Although the term Repressive Self is a psychological name I have coined, for thousands of years people have been familiar with the negative emotions which make up the Repressive Self: fear, shyness, inadequacy, sadness. Through the years people have been using their own trial-and-error methods to try to free themselves from these painful feelings.

Since the Rev. Norman Vincent Peale's book, *The Power of Positive Thinking*, appeared in 1937, many people have tried to use this method to overcome the negative emotions that hamper their personalities. If they feel inadequate in certain situations, they try to "think positively." They imagine themselves feeling confident and at ease. A salesman, afraid to call on potential customers, "thinks positively" and imagines himself striding into the customer's office, radiating confidence, and making the sale. Dr. Peale's readers have been patting themselves encouragingly on the back and swearing that *this* time they're going to do it. Unfortunately, positive thinking works for only a few very strong-willed people. It does not work at all for the great majority.

The reason that positive thinking does not work for most people is that it is not strong enough to deal with the powerful, unconscious emotions which stem from childhood. Positive thinking is like putting a Band-Aid on a severed artery and then wondering why the blood continues to spurt. Or to use another kind of analogy, it is like putting on someone else's expensive suit in order to give the impression of being wealthy, but it is still your same old anxious self walking around inside it.

During my years as a consulting psychologist, I have had numerous patients who had earlier tried to use positive thinking to cure their shyness, their fears, their sexual inhibitions, their feeling of inadequacy, their depressions, and their lack of self-confidence. When positive thinking did not work, instead of suspecting there was something wrong with the method, they came to the conclusion there was something wrong with them! Typically they would tell me: "I've tried so hard to think positively and get over my shyness, but it doesn't work. I guess I just don't have enough faith!" So I explain that the fault lies not in them but in the technique they have been trying to use. Then I describe something that does work, a method I call *negative thinking*. It is important to understand negative thinking because it is a powerful tool in your efforts to gain freedom from your Repressive Self.

Negative thinking came into being many years ago when a psychologist named Dr. Knight Dunlap was learning to type at age thirty-five. He consistently made a simple but irritating little error. He meant to type "t-h-e" for "the," but instead he repeatedly typed "h-t-e." Almost anybody else would simply have tried harder to type the proper letters. If he had been a devotee of "positive thinking," he would have pictured the right letters in his mind and imagined himself typing them. But Dr. Dunlap tried a different approach. Being experimentally minded, he tried this little experiment —he deliberately typed the mistake. He purposely typed "h-t-e" about 175 or 200 times, at the same time acknowledging that this was a mistake. After he stopped deliberately typing the mistake, he found he could type "t-h-e" without any difficulty.

How did this work? Remember, Dr. Dunlap wanted *consciously* to type "t-h-e," but against his conscious control "h-t-e" kept coming out. He took what was involuntarily and unconsciously coming out of him ("h-t-e") and placed it under his voluntary and conscious control. After he had voluntarily practiced a number of times what he did *not* want to do (the mistake), he then found he had psychologically mastered the negative habit. Dr. Dunlap called his discovery "negative practice." He found it could be used with the learning of all sorts of muscular coordination skills such as typing, sending Morse code, swimming, golf, etc. By practicing the mistake, you learn to break the power of the mistake over you.

What I call the technique of negative thinking

is an expansion of Dr. Dunlap's negative practice into the field of human feelings and emotions. Here's how I have been using it in my therapy practice.

A few years ago a young man consulted me because he had a great fear of flying. Unfortunately for him, his work demanded that he do a good deal of air travel. He was literally terrified every time he went to an airport. He would sit on the plane and be miserable from the moment he got on until he got off. He would start worrying a few days before a trip and feel shaky for a few days after.

He was one of those who had tried positive thinking to solve his problems. In fact, when he came to me as a patient, he had tried it for a year, but it had done nothing for him. He would picture to himself a "positive," pleasant trip, free of worry and anxiety. He would imagine how clear the skies were and how beautiful the plane looked soaring through the air. He would say to himself: "You will be safer up in the airplane than if you were down on the Los Angeles freeways." (This was true, incidentally, but it did absolutely nothing to help him get over his terror of flying!)

The first thing I did after he came to me for treatment was to convince him to stop trying to conquer his problem through positive thinking.

Then I gave him a thorough battery of psychological tests to find out what was behind his fear of flying. I discovered he was chock-full of guilt feelings. He had become successful in his work through a series of business maneuvers that, although technically legal, ran counter to the strict religious upbringing he had had as a boy. Because of his enormous load of guilt, he had a great need to punish himself. Underlying his fear of flying was his unconscious wish that the airplane would crash so that he would be punished by being hurt or killed. In this respect his irrational fear of flying was typical of the irrational fears of many people. A conscious irrational *fear* often turns out to be an unconscious *wish*. He was *subconsciously* wishing for punishment while *consciously* fearing it.

Helping my patient find out *why* he was afraid of flying was only the first step in curing him. Merely knowing *why* still left him as fearful as ever when he entered an air terminal. So I instructed him in the technique of negative thinking. Here is what I told him: "When you are driving to the airport, deliberately exaggerate all your feelings that you are a guilty person who should be punished by having the airplane crash. Tell yourself: 'I am the most evil person in the world. I don't deserve to live. Only by having the airplane crash can I make up for my sins and misdeeds.' "

He was told to repeat the same things to himself in the air terminal and during the trip. I told him to really "ham it up," and go all out in criticizing and vilifying himself.

It would be nice to report that the first time he used negative thinking he realized how untrue and ridiculous it was for him to feel this way and that the next day he hopped on a plane completely at ease. But subconscious emotions are deeply ingrained, and that's why we don't get instant miracles when dealing with human feelings. It took time—three months in his case—but he was finally able to overcome his fear of flying.

How did this technique work? When silent messages from our unconscious mind are sent to us, we are powerless against them, no matter how irrational they are. (Clearly it is irrational to believe that you are such a guilty person that an airplane should crash, just so you can be punished!) But when these silent messages are brought up into the conscious mind and put into words, they lose their power over us. This does not happen right away. But over a period of time we realize *on a gut feeling level* how ridiculous it is to let ourselves be pushed around and dominated by these irrational, negative feelings.

Physicians use a biological term "homeostasis," denoting a "steady state" in the body. Homeostasis means that in our physical bodies there is a drive toward health, toward restoring the body to a steady state, whenever something goes wrong. For example, if your blood sugar level becomes too low, automatic biochemical processes go into action to bring up the blood sugar to its normal level.

Much of the time we tend to think that a physician "does something" to us when he cures us of some physical affliction. In many cases this is not true. What he has done is to assist the homeostatic healing processes of nature. The physician merely clears certain things out of the way to set the stage for the curative powers of nature to take over. When a doctor sets a broken leg, it is nature, not the doctor, who knits the broken bones together.

Many people are not aware of the fact that just as there is a biological healing process in our bodies, there is also a drive toward psychological health in our minds. Within each individual there are powerful growth forces, part of our Potential Self, which are striving toward self-actualization. These forces are continually moving us in the direction of greater self-acceptance, independence, and the ability to express all of our capacities and potentialities to the fullest.

But these growth forces can be hindered by unconscious messages from the past, silent negative communications from our invisible parents. We need to make these unconscious messages conscious. When we use negative thinking, our rational mind can realize on a feeling level how ridiculous it is to be held in bondage to the past. That is how we clear the way for the growth forces of our Potential Self to take over. What the biological process of homeostasis is to our body, the psychological growth forces of the Potential Self are to our mind.

In other words, negative thinking is a process by which the negative emotions of your Repressor (fear, inhibitions, inadequacy, depression) can be cleared away, allowing the positive growth forces of your Potential Self to begin to work. Let me describe some more cases from my files to show you how this works. (Incidentally, when I use cases from my clinical practice for illustrative purposes, I always change identities and circumstances so that the person's privacy is protected.)

A twenty-seven-year-old girl, a clerk in an office, once came to see me because of general feelings of shyness, inadequacy, and difficulty in meeting people. In the early course of her therapy she stated in one interview that she knew she was not very bright but that was "a cross she would just have to bear." I knew this was not true, just from talking to her, but in order to convince her I gave her an intelligence test.

She scored at the eighty-third percentile, meaning she was smarter than 82 out of 100 people. The naive laymen might think she would have been delighted when I broke the news to her. Not so. Not so at all. She didn't believe the test results. She actually thought I had doctored the test scores to make her look more intelligent than she really was!

This meant we needed to delve into the psychological reasons why she had difficulty believing the evidence of the intelligence test. The reasons were not hard to find. Her mother had constantly disparaged and belittled her from the time she was a little girl. "Stupid" was one of more common words her mother used to describe her. "You're stupid," she would say, or "That was a stupid thing to do," or "Can't you ever do anything right?"

Consequently, the girl had taken over her mother's evaluation of herself. Deep down she believed she was stupid and unintelligent. We were working on other things in her therapy as well, but on this particular problem I taught her to use negative thinking. I explained that in reality she was intelligent, as proved objectively by the intelligence test scores. But she kept receiving silent belittling messages from the mother in her mind. We had to bring out these silent messages loud and clear so that she could realize with her innermost feelings how wrong they were.

She lived by herself in an apartment, so I instructed her to spend five minutes every morning looking in the mirror and deliberately exaggerating, in a negative-thinking fashion, the messages of her invisible mother. I told her to look at herself and say the single word "stupid" over and over again, hundreds of times, until it lost its meaning as a word, and became just a meaningless jumble of sounds.

I suggested that whenever she was by herself—driving her car, in her apartment, out for a walk, riding her bicycle—she was to use negative thinking and exaggerate the put-down messages her mother had sent her. As you might suspect, the message that she was stupid was not the only negative message she had received. She had also come to feel she was dull and uninteresting and could never attract a man. These attitudes took time to change, because, as I explained to her, "Your mother had literally thousands of *anti*-therapeutic consultations with you when you were growing up, and I have only one therapeutic consultation with you every week."

Over a period of time, remarkable changes took place in this girl. She began to feel that she really *was* intelligent and realized she was capable of much more than being just a file clerk. She enrolled in secretarial courses at night school, and some time later got a job as a legal secretary. She began to dress fashionably and wear makeup. She looked vastly different from the pale, mousy, creature who first walked into my office. About a year after starting therapy she acquired a boyfriend, and from then on her self-confidence began to increase by giant strides.

This case illustrates how the use of negative thinking involves the deliberate exaggeration of negative messages sent by parents. The negative messages were originally sent by the real parents of the patient's childhood. But now that the patient is an adult they are sent by the invisible parents inside the patient's mind. Sometimes it's not enough to exaggerate the negative parental messages; the patient also needs to carry on a dialogue with the invisible parents. The next case illustrates this.

This was a thirty-two-year-old married woman with a two-and-one-half-year-old boy. She consulted me because her young, rambunctious son was driving her up the wall. She was a woman who prided herself on her housekeeping, and in the first years of her marriage before her child was born, she took great pride in keeping a spotless house. But when her son became a toddler and a creative, energetic, free spirit, things changed drastically. She felt that she spent most of her days trying to clean up the mess he made of the house. She was worn out because as soon as she'd clean, he would mess up. She could never keep anything tidy. She was beginning to lose her temper badly with him and became terrified that she would do him some real harm.

Going back into her family history, I found that her mother had been a fanatical housekeeper, who spent every spare minute washing, scrubbing, and polishing all parts of the house until you could almost literally eat off the floor. Even so, her mother's housekeeping was not good enough for her father. He was the kind of man who, as soon as he came home from work, would go over to a cabinet and run his finger over the top of it. If dust came off, he would exclaim with a triumphant gleam in his eye: "Dust! Is that the best you can do when you have all day to keep this house clean?"

I pointed out to my patient that she was receiving silent negative messages from both her parents. Her mother was sending this message: "You must keep your house absolutely spotless or you are a failure as a wife and mother. You must keep your house as immaculate as I tried to keep mine." Her father was sending this message: "I can't love or respect a woman who doesn't keep a house that measures up to my standards of 100 percent perfection. I will not love you if your house does not measure up as it should." Obviously she could not satisfy the housekeeping demands of her invisible mother and father with a normal getting-into-everything two-and-one-half-year-old boy around the house.

I told her I had written two books on child raising and read to her from one describing the typical behavior of a normal two-and-one-half-year-old. She admitted that the description fitted her son perfectly, but added: "I don't care if he is normal. *I* can't stand it!" As she spoke, she could hear that she was acting more like her mother than she wanted to. I explained negative thinking to her and told her to imagine she was her mother speaking.

"Imagine that's your mother sitting on that chair over there," I told her. "What is she saying to you?"

"Oh, I know," she said, "my mother's telling me that I'm not doing a good enough job. *She'd* never let the baby get away with what I let him get away with. She'd lock him in his room so he couldn't mess up the house."

"Now," I encouraged her, "you be the mother. Tell your daughter more. Exaggerate."

"You'll never be as good a housekeeper as I am," she said angrily. "You're such a disappointment to me. I tried so hard to teach you the right things."

She continued in this vein, until I interrupted her. "Now imagine you're your father."

She thought for a moment. "I'm actually turning over in my grave when I see how slovenly you've become. I feel sorry for your husband. You'd better be careful he doesn't leave you. I'm actually glad I'm dead so I won't have to visit your filthy house."

It took a while for my patient to understand that she was trying to please her invisible parents by living up to their ideas about cleanliness. Her Repressive Self had been tying her down by forcing her to conform to their unrealistic standards. Luckily for her, she had at least one positive factor going for her in her current life situation. Her husband was not at all like her father, for he had reasonable rather than unreasonable expectations of her.

After she had considerable practice in upbraiding herself for being a terrible housekeeper, I instructed her to begin answering back the exaggerated demands of her invisible parents. I told her to say things like: "I'm actually a very good housekeeper. No one could be a perfect housekeeper with a two-and-one-half-year-old boy around. If my father had to try to keep house with a two-and-one-half-year-old in the place, he'd go bananas!" Basically I was teaching her to have a dialogue with her invisible parents, answering their unreasonable demands by telling them what was realistically possible.

Of course, there were many other things she found difficult to handle in the behavior of her little boy. We worked on this in her therapy, as I taught her better ways of coping with his behavior. But negative thinking was the main technique I used to help her diminish the impossible demands she made upon herself to be a perfect housekeeper. After using negative thinking and the dialogue with her invisible parents, she began to realize that she was basically a good housekeeper, who was doing all that anyone could reasonably expect with a young toddler in the house. As she became able to view the situation in this light, she did not get so upset at the various normal things her little boy did which prevented her from keeping a 100 percent spotless house.

Sometimes there are situations where another person such as your spouse can be of help to you in using negative thinking to tear down part of your Repressive Self. The next case illustrates this.

A thirty-five-year-old woman, married twelve years, came in with her husband for marriage counseling. Basically what had been happening in their marriage was what I call "sweeping it under the rug." Various sorts of problems and conflicts between them that should have been brought out into the open, faced, and resolved, had instead been swept under the marital rug. Finally the conflicts could not be ignored any longer. The tension between the couple had become unbearable and the problems had to be faced. The particular example I am going to mention here was only one of a number of problems that needed work in their marriage. But I am focusing on it because I taught them negative thinking as their main technique to use in overcoming it.

The wife was inhibited in many ways in their sexual relationship. Her husband had put up with her fears and inhibitions for twelve years, but he was not about to put up with them any longer. One particular thing seemed to sum up his sexual complaints. For many years he had been trying to get his wife to join him in having oral sex. With respect to oral sex, she would allow him to "go down" on her, but she could not bring herself to "go down" on him. The husband was terribly angered at what he called "this one-sided deal." He complained, "She'll let me do it to her, but she won't do it to me." He told me: "I know lots of guys whose wives do it, and I don't see any reason why she can't. I want some variety in our sex!"

There were other ways in which his wife was inhibited sexually, but her inhibitions on oral sex seemed to be the thing that particularly infuriated her husband and soured him on all other aspects of their sexual relationship. I felt that if we could break through this barrier, it would facilitate the solving of other conflicts. Of course, we were simultaneously working on many nonsexual problems, but as far as sex was concerned, I decided to work on oral sex first. But not directly, to begin with.

I had taken the life history of both wife and husband. The wife had grown up in a very Victorian family in which sex was hush-hush, never mentioned. She had not even been prepared for menstruation by her mother but had found out in a haphazard manner from her older sister. Her whole sex instruction had consisted of dire and vague warnings from her mother, when she was a teenager, to "watch out for boys" because "they all have one thing on their mind" and they might "do bad things to you." So it was pretty clear that she was receiving silent antisex messages from her invisible parents, particularly her mother.

I did not begin directly with oral sex but led up to it gradually, proceeding gently, because of her massive fears and inhibitions. I began by instructing her and her husband in the "pleasuring" techniques first pioneered by the sex experts Dr. Masters and Johnson. I told them they should spend fifteen to twenty minutes each night pleasuring each other. I explained that this was not to be thought of as a prelude to sexual intercourse (although if it did happen to lead to intercourse, that was all right). The purpose of the pleasuring sessions was simply for each of them to learn to give and receive pleasure by stroking and caressing each other's bodies. They could do this with the help of various oils, lotions, baby powder, or they could use nothing at all. After some experimentation, they chose baby powder. They were instructed simply to caress and fondle each other all over their bodies and to experiment with different types of strokes and caresses.

This was an entirely new experience for both of them, and it not only furnished the beginning for a new and improved sexual relationship, but also gave them a simple and nonverbal way of saying to the other: "I care about you."

After about two months of using the pleasuring techniques, I felt it was time to bring up the matter of oral sex. I first saw the wife alone, since she found it a very difficult topic to discuss.

I broached the subject cautiously, hoping she would be able to talk about her husband's feelings about it. Finally, she said, very self-consciously, "He wants me to kiss him—down there."

"Oral sex?" I asked.

She nodded, almost blushing. "My husband has been after me to do it for years, but there's no sense discussing it, because I simply can't do it."

I told her I would not allow her to state the problem that way, because it was incorrect. I said, "When you say you *can't* do it, that implies there is some force outside of you so overwhelmingly powerful that you cannot engage in oral sex. That simply is not true.

"You are locating the problem outside yourself, where you have no responsibility for it, instead of inside yourself, where you do have responsibility and *can* potentially do something about it. So it is not true to say you *can't* do it. There is nothing outside of you to prevent you from allowing your husband to put his penis in your mouth. Instead of saying 'I can't do it,' try to say 'I won't do it because I'm afraid.'" She reluctantly agreed that what I said was a basically correct view of the situation.

Then she went on, "But I'm certainly not going to do a thing like that, because only prostitutes do that." I asked her, "Where did you get that impression?"

It turned out that when she was a teen-ager, some friends were giggling about something they called "sixty-nine." She was very naive, and when she asked what they meant, they wouldn't tell her. So the next day she asked her mother. Her mother was shocked and angry. "Who told you about that?" her mother demanded. She still didn't know what it meant, but she realized immediately she should never have asked. She told her mother it was some girls she didn't know, and that she had just overheard them talking.

"Well, let me tell you, young lady," her mother said, "no self-respecting woman would ever do a dirty thing like that. Only prostitutes would do such a despicable thing."

As gently as I could I explained to her that this was not true. I quoted various sexual studies to her to show that a large percentage of husbands and wives use oral sex. I said that if her husband had no desire for it, then her negative attitudes would cause no problem. They could go through the rest of their married lives without it. But, I pointed out, that was not the case. To her husband, her hang-ups on oral sex seemed to sum up all of her sexual inhibitions that bothered and frustrated him.

I told her that each of them had various ways in which they wanted the other to change in order to make the marriage relationship more satisfactory. This was one way in which he very much wanted her to change. I said that if she could learn to change her sexual attitudes, I felt sure it would have a very positive effect on her husband and would motivate him to change in other ways which were important to her. I had to do quite a bit of persuading to get her to see that it would potentially *benefit her* in other ways if she could learn to be more free about oral sex. Finally, she reluctantly agreed to give it a try.

First I taught her to use negative thinking and to deliberately exaggerate what she imagined her mother and father would think about her taking her husband's penis in her mouth. Then I found out she was fond of sweet things. So I told her to take part of a doughnut, a candy cane, or an ice cream cone (all of which she liked) and imagine it was her husband's penis. She was to say things to herself such as: "That's vile and disgusting. Only a prostitute or a despicable woman would do such a filthy thing."

When I felt she had practiced sufficiently by herself, I enlisted her husband's help. I explained to him about negative thinking. I told him how his wife was still a captive—in her own mind—of her Repressive Self and the antisexual messages of her invisible parents. I outlined how he and his wife could work together, using negative thinking, to enable her to loosen up her sexual hang-ups.

I told the two of them that our ultimate goal was for her to be able to have full and complete oral sex with her husband. But we had to begin with where she was now, psychologically speaking, which was that she was reluctant even to put her husband's penis in her mouth. I explained the basic ground rule of the technique: whenever she got to feeling anxious or uneasy about what they were doing, they were to stop immediately and do no more that night. This relieved her right away, for she realized she would never be pressured into doing something she did not want to do or was not yet ready to do.

Then I explained to both of them that the "lessons in oral sex," like the pleasuring sessions, were not to be thought of as leading up to sexual intercourse, although if they did, that was all right. They were told to begin by taking off their clothes and being naked in bed together. Then she was to use negative thinking, deliberately exaggerating what her parents might say, such as: "Look at Bert's penis. It's an ugly looking thing. It would be disgusting and repulsive for you to take it into your mouth." Then Bert was to chime in in the same vein: "Martha, only a whore would do such a terrible thing as take my penis in her mouth. You are a pure, clean woman, and I know you would never do a thing like that."

After the two of them had practiced this for a few weeks, I had them move on to another phase. Now I had Bert coat his penis with things such as marmalade, strawberry jam, and whipped cream. (I know this is going to seem weird and far-out to some of you reading this, but let me remind you of the immortal words of that famous Hungarian philosopher Zsa Zsa Gabor: "If you haven't tried it, don't knock it!"). The wife was instructed to continue the negative thinking, while at the same time licking the goodies off her husband's penis. And it worked! The pleasant sensations she was getting from her tongue counteracted the negative things she was saying out loud about how repulsive it was to put her husband's penis in her mouth.

Of course, there were setbacks in this process. The wife's old feelings that she was acting like a prostitute and a "dirty woman" came back from time to time. Whenever that happened, the two of them would immediately stop what they were doing for that night. It took around seven or eight months for the wife to be able to engage in full and complete oral sex relations with her husband.

When that finally happened, the husband was like a kid in a candy store. He was so happy he spontaneously brought her flowers and took her out to dinner the next night. Since one of her complaints about him was that he never did spontaneous romantic things like that, she was delighted. And, of course, at an unconscious level, this motivated her to further loosen up her Victorian sexual attitudes. In the course of over twenty years of marriage counseling, I can't recall offhand a more grateful husband. He said to me a few weeks later, "You're expensive, Doc, but believe me, it's the best money I've ever spent!"

Once again, negative thinking had proved to be a most valuable technique in helping a person break loose from the deeply ingrained negative attitudes of her Repressive Self.

I have described these cases to show you how negative thinking has worked in a variety of situations to enable people to free themselves from their Repressor and begin to get in touch with their Potential Self. I have told you what kind of instructions I as a therapist have given my patients to teach them the use of negative thinking. You can also use negative thinking to break loose from your Repressor.

The types of problems which can be attacked and solved by means of negative thinking are quite extensive. Here are some examples:

Are you afraid of:

asking for a raise?

walking into a roomful of people where you know only a few?

standing up to someone?

expressing angry feelings?

asking someone for a date?

giving a speech?

talking to strangers?

entering into a relationship with the opposite sex, for fear of getting hurt?

a dictatorial parent?

a domineering spouse?

Most important of all, are you afraid of *being yourself* . . . the person deep within you . . . your Potential Self . . . the you that could be?

In this chapter I have described what negative thinking is and how and why it works. In the next chapter I will show you the specific steps you must take in learning to use negative thinking to solve your problems.

5. *Getting Rid Of Your Repressive Self*

You now understand which type of Repressive Self is inhibiting you and that you need to overcome this before you can become your Potential Self. It isn't easy. But it can be done. This chapter will show you how to use the technique of Negative Thinking to do this.

Using negative thinking by yourself is quite different from using it with a therapist to assist you. If you suffer from a terrible fear of flying, heights, or any other severe emotional problem, you will not get "total relief" from reading a book or doing psychological exercises.

Severe and deeply entrenched problems that peo-

ple have require the skills of a professional therapist to help solve them. If this applies to you, or
if you even think it may, I suggest you now turn
to Chapter 10, "If You Need Professional Help,"
and mull it over.

The technique of negative thinking is intended
to help you free yourself gradually from the type
of Repressive Self which is holding you down.
During this process, you may also "hook into"
other specific problems that have troubled you,
such as shyness with the opposite sex or a fear of
speaking in public. Such problems may gradually
dissolve under the technique of negative thinking
also.

But right now I want to emphasize using this
technique as a weapon against your type of Repressor. For instance, suppose you are basically an
appeaser. You have just received a letter from
Cousin Bernice that she and her husband George,
the three kids and two dogs are planning to visit
you for a couple of weeks.

You are not overjoyed to receive this news. You
wish you could tell them not to come, but that's
out of the question. It isn't hard to define your
problem: you are feeling imposed on. You don't
want these particular relatives to visit, but outright
refusal will create family problems.

Here's how to use the technique of negative thinking. You are sitting in the living room by yourself. Imagine that in the chair in front of you sits your Repressive Self. Your job is to play the role of this Repressor. The things your Repressive Self says to you are usually silent and unconscious. And because they *are* silent and unconscious, they influence your thinking powerfully, no matter how irrational they are. Your job is to say aloud what your Repressive Self is thinking. When you actually hear the words, you can more effectively fight the self-defeating message. As you act out your Repressive Self, deliberately exaggerate all of the demands made on you. Lay it on thick.

"I don't deny that having Bernice, George, and the kids to visit will be a terrible strain. But so what? They're your mother's favorite relatives. It would be unthinkable to refuse them.

"What if you do have a lot of extra cooking? You did it the last time they were here and it didn't ruin you, did it?

"What if they are the world's champion subtle complainers? Can't you put up with that for only two weeks? Remember their last visit! They complained, oh ever so subtly, about your cooking and the places you and your husband took them to visit. There wasn't anything they wholeheartedly enjoyed.

116

"But you've just got to put up with it. If you don't, they'll complain to your mother. And the last thing in the world you want is to antagonize your mother. You don't dare stick up for yourself and what *you* want. Be a doormat and let other people impose on you as you have all your life. You're just stuck with it. Put on the best face you can, and go ahead. You can't possibly refuse them. You're just stuck! stuck! stuck! There is no civilized way you can get out of it."

That's the way your Repressor would speak. That's the way your Repressor has spoken to you all your life in any conflict between what *you* want and what somebody else wants. Now you are going to learn to talk back to your Repressive Self. You now know that you have repressed the part of your personality that enables you to stand up for yourself and to do what is good for *you*.

You could talk back to your Repressive Self in this fashion: "I absolutely refuse to let myself in for a miserable two weeks when I can avoid it, just by saying 'no.' The last time Bernice and George and the kids came was a nightmare. I was counting the days till they left. I had a lot of headaches and most of them were probably psychosomatic.

"I've got to admit that part of it was my own fault. They did offer to stay at a motel, even though they didn't sound like they meant it. But I would have felt too guilty letting them do that. So noble me, I was the one who insisted they stay with us.

"If I'm honest with myself, I know it just won't work out for them to stay here. It would be a miserable repeat of the last time.

"I know what to do. I can write to Bernice that we'd love to see her but that it just isn't convenient for her to stay here this time. I can invite her over for a few dinners. That I can stand. But it's just plain crazy for me to invite the entire family to stay with us for two weeks when I know the total effect will be to make me miserable."

This, of course, is only a summarized version of a negative thinking dialogue between your Repressor and part of your emerging Potential Self. You may need several such dialogues to get over your fears of standing up for yourself.

If Bernice feels insulted, that is her problem, not yours. *She* will have to figure out what to do about you, since you have already figured out what to do about her.

Go ahead and write the letter. You'll feel guilty about it—so expect that. After years of being a doormat, you are not going to change completely in the brief time it takes to write a letter. However, you will have taken a strong and positive step in asserting yourself and your rights. You will see that the world does not come crashing down when you dare to say "no" to somebody. In fact, it's rather exciting to learn to stand up for yourself. And the next time it will be easier to say "I'd rather not."

Now is the time for you to do the following psychological exercise. Take a half-hour when you can be alone. Think back over your life. Jot down times when you have agreed to do something that you didn't really want to do. Or a time when somebody imposed on you or took advantage of your good nature.

Then pick one situation. Take the time to alternately play the roles of your Repressive Self and your emerging Potential Self, as described in the previous scenario. Have a dialogue between the two selves. Above all, really "ham it up." Exaggerate the demands of your Repressive Self that you be a doormat and not stand up for yourself because you would "hurt other people's feelings." Throw in a touch of humor if you feel like it to show how ridiculous the demands of your Repressor are.

Save the list of situations you have jotted down, and at your convenience, role-play each one, first as your Repressor, then as your emerging Potential Self.

When you have done this for a time and really

have the feel of role-playing, try to become aware of *current* situations, where you are tempted to give in and do what someone else wants, even though you'd rather not. Then role-play these situations. See if you can learn to assert yourself in experiences that are a part of your *present* life. These, of course, will be more difficult for you, because they are not over and done with. As part of your present existence, they are very real. But keep at it, and slowly you will find your Repressor losing its hold over you. Gradually you will discover the ability to stand up for yourself, and the exhilarating feeling that goes along with it.

Now let's shift to a different scenario. Your type is the aggressor. You are a salesperson, a successful one. For the last two years you have led your company in sales. You've won the annual sales contest both years. Now a new contest is in progress, and you want to make it three in a row.

But something's starting to go wrong. You can sense it. You know you're leaning too hard on your customers. You can't relax. But how could you? It's important to win. To you, it's very important. You can't even let yourself consider not winning.

Still the nagging fear persists. Like a throbbing toothache, it throws you off your stride. And once you've lost your pace, you try even harder and get more tense. The more tense you become, the more difficult it is to make sales. It's a real vicious circle, and it's starting to make you feel sick inside. There's a gnawing pain in your stomach and you're starting to have frequent headaches. Everything gets on your nerves. You yell at people you don't want to. It's a real mess and you don't know what to do.

Here's one thing you can do. You can try negative thinking. You are feeling tense and nervous, and your fear about winning the sales contest is what is triggering it. You are now ready to confront your Repressive Self. As you take on the role of Repressor, here are some things you might say:

"You're beginning to blow it, Charlie. You know you've *got* to win this contest. If you don't, what will people think? What will everybody say? You know what they'll say, but not to you directly, of course: 'Old Charlie's slipping.'

"And they'll be right. You are slipping. If you can't win a contest like this, that you've already won in the past, what right have you to call yourself a salesman? If you don't win this contest, you're a *failure*, that's what you are. Why don't you at least be honest and call yourself by your right name? Failure, failure, failure!

"And what will Janice and the kids think? They'll know you've lost your grip and you can't cut it anymore when it comes to supporting your family. You know how disappointed the twins will be if you don't give them a car for a graduation present this June—all because you didn't win the contest!

"And the boss? If the worst really happens, he may even fire you! He's counting on you to boost the sales of all the other men. You're a key figure in the sales force and you'll be letting everybody down. You've been lucky enough to make it in the past, but right now you've got to look at yourself honestly and admit you're nothing but a failure!"

When you play the role of Repressive Self, exaggerate the fear of failure. And if you feel like it, leaven your exaggeration with a little humor.

Now you need to speak with the voice of your Potential Self, answering some of these wild accusations your Repressor is hurling at you.

"Three months after the contest results are announced, who's going to remember last year's winner except last year's winner? That first year I won the contest I couldn't remember who had won it the year before. It will be the same way this year. Nobody will care who won after it's over. They're wrapped up in themselves and their own concerns.

All they care about is whether they win. And if I don't win, they're not going to waste time looking down their noses at me.

"As for the boss, whether I win this particular contest or not, he knows for a fact that I'm his best salesman, year in and year out. He's certainly not going to fire his top salesman! And who says the twins *have* to have a car for graduation? Not all kids get them, by any means. If we don't have the money, I won't be able to get them a car and that's it. If they want it badly enough, they can get part-time jobs and earn it themselves.

"And Janice? She's said a thousand times she wishes I wouldn't work so hard. She'd like to see more of me and have me spend more time with the family.

"Apparently it boils down to my mother and father and their high expectations that I would get top grades, be president of my class, and things like that. They never said it in so many words, but I seemed to get the message: 'We will love you if you are successful, son. But you must always be successful to keep our love.' Well, I've got to learn to stop pushing myself in order to please them. As far as Janice is concerned, I'm plenty successful as I am. I'm sure that Janice loves me just for me.

"All of a sudden, the contest doesn't seem to

be quite as important as it did earlier. Sure, I'd still like to win. Winning is always better than losing. But now, somehow, losing doesn't seem to hold all the psychological horrors it did a little while ago."

So much for the scenario of a typical aggressor. Now let's turn to the retreater. Imagine you've been dating Alice for almost two years. You get along well in all aspects: intellectually, emotionally, and physically. Your interests are similar and you really enjoy each other's company. As far as you're concerned, there is no reason why this arrangement shouldn't continue just the way it is. But Alice sees things differently. She wants the security of marriage.

She first mentioned it about six months ago. You told her you'd think it over and you did. Now and then. But you didn't come to any conclusion. Then, finally, there was that terrible scene at her place.

"I'm sick and tired of your sitting on the fence!" she shouted. It's unusual for Alice to shout, but she did that time. "You've got to make up your mind whether you want me or not, because I'm not going to settle for going steady for twenty years!"

You hate ultimatums! And Alice knows it. In fact, you were almost tempted to tell her if that's how she felt, then forget it! Only you can't forget it, because you really do care about her. But marriage? That's a real commitment. Are you ready for that? You don't know. You tossed and turned much of the night trying to decide.

Your problem is that you have to make a decision whether to get married or not. But you need negative thinking to help you solve this. So imagine your Repressive Self sitting across from you and saying things like this:

"Freedom is the key word here. Right now you've got your freedom and you've got Alice too. She would really leave it that way if she were the right kind of person for you. But she won't. She's pushing for marriage, like all women do, sooner or later. And marriage is a trap. It means you're committed to live with this woman and only this woman the rest of your life. What could be more of a trap than that? That's a total lack of freedom, and nothing is more important than your freedom.

"It's unfair of Alice to try to pin you down. Why can't she be as flexible as you are? Right now, you've got just about the right emotional distance from Alice. Close enough, but not too close.

"But here she is asking you for a commitment. And commitments are psychologically dangerous. When you make an emotional commitment to someone, you risk being hurt. Think of the people

125

who have hurt you in the past. Why take the risk? You've got a good job. You've got relationships with enough people so that you're not bored or lonely. Why stick your neck out with the close relationship that marriage involves? Don't fall into the marriage trap. Stay footloose and fancy-free."

Now you can begin to answer your Repressive Self.

"You're right; marriage *can* be a trap, but it doesn't have to be. With the wrong person it is, no question about that. But Alice isn't like anybody I've ever known before. She doesn't make a lot of demands on me. Even though presenting me with an ultimatum is out of character for her, she does have to be concerned for her own future. And I kind of admire her for looking out for herself.

"But the most important thing is that all my life I've been afraid to get close to people, due to you, my Repressive Self. You've taught me only too well that the only way I can avoid being hurt by people is to keep my emotional distance from them. That may be true, but I also lose chances for a great deal of happiness when I avoid closeness. Well, here's a chance for real closeness with Alice, and I'm not going to lose it because of the fears you have planted in me. Sure, if I make a commitment to Alice through marriage and really get close to her, I take a risk. But I'd be taking a worse risk if I let a girl like Alice get away. I'm not going to listen to your fear-talk any more, Repressive Self. I'm going to take the risk and marry her!'"

The examples I have sketched may be quite different from situations in which you find yourself. But the technique of negative thinking remains the same. Try to practice about fifteen minutes each day. That's not a great deal of time to set aside for work which is important for the development of your full personality potential. At first the use of negative thinking will probably be difficult. You are fighting against deeply entrenched mechanisms which have warped your personality potential in the direction of being an appeaser, an aggressor, or a retreater. But keep at it and you will begin to see changes in yourself. Where there was rigidity of personality, you will begin to see an increased openness to new ways of responding.

Chapter 3 described the various defense mechanisms used by your Repressive Self to keep you unaware of certain feelings going on inside you. Not being aware of these feelings puts you at a disadvantage in dealing with other people. Because our defense mechanisms operate unconsciously, many of them are hard to detect. In fact, as you read that chapter, I'll wager you probably thought much more about various people you know and *their* defense mechanisms than you thought about yourself and your own defense mechanisms.

Here is one way you can unearth your own defense mechanisms and do something about them. Mannerisms that irritate us in other people usually reflect parts of our own personality that are unconsciously troubling us. One of the stingiest men I know always complains how everyone else is a tightwad. A woman who is almost totally self-centered complains how thoughtless people are. A man who drives as if he were the only person on the road grouses about "road hogs."

When you find someone else acting in ways that really bug you, consider the possibility that these ways are a part of *your own* personality that you have hidden from yourself. Then try negative thinking to deliberately exaggerate this way of thinking or acting and see if any of it fits you.

If we did not feel psychologically impelled to use defense mechanisms, we would be aware of *all* of the feelings that are going on within ourselves and be able to tolerate them. Most people do the exact opposite. If they find negative feelings within themselves, such as anger, sadness, fear, or hurt, they try as quickly as possible to get rid of these uncomfortable feelings. Unfortunately, this drives the negative feelings underground and makes it harder for the person to get rid of them. Instead, our motto should be: *don't fight the negative feelings.* Let yourself drift with the current of your feelings. There is a limit to how long a negative feeling will persist, if you do not oppose it.

Feelings you do not fight go away sooner than feelings you fight. As you learn to let your feelings flow, you will develop a basic confidence in your ability to handle *all* the feelings which you encounter in life. It's as if you can say to yourself: "Hey, all these feelings are me. . . . I'm loving and warm and joyful and playful and sexy. But I'm also sad and depressed and angry and hurt and fearful and inadequate. And I'm strong enough to allow myself to accept the fullness of all these feelings, because all of them are part of me. I don't need to be so afraid of my feelings that I am compelled to block them out with defense mechanisms."

Once you begin to enjoy this kind of security you will develop a great deal of confidence in your ability to handle almost any situation. You will know that *all* of your feelings, negative as well as positive, may be used by your Potential Self to cope with whatever circumstances may confront you.

6: You Must Be Born Again

In my opinion, Jesus of Nazareth was the most profound psychologist of all time. I find it striking that psychologists have neglected one of his most penetrating observations on human personality: "You must be born again." Jesus said this to a man named Nicodemus, who responded, in amazement, "How can a man be born again when he is old? Can he enter a second time into his mother's womb and be born again?"[1]

Jesus made other similar statements, which were equally puzzling to those whose thinking was rigid: "Unless you become like a little child, you cannot

1. John 3:4

enter into the kingdom of heaven,"[2] and "The kingdom of heaven is within you."[3]

Statements like these have been subject to varying interpretations throughout the ages. As I understand these words of Jesus, He is saying precisely what I am discussing in this book. There was a time when your Potential Self was fully functioning, when as a little toddler, you were full of self-confidence and eager to explore the wondrous world around you. But now this spontaneous and free little child has been imprisoned by the rigid armoring of the Repressive Self. Therefore, your central personality task, whatever your age, is psychologically to be "born again," to become like a little child so that you can find the kingdom of heaven within you. In psychological terms we call this your Potential Self.

The key question is: how do I do this? At this point may I suggest that merely to *read* the rest of this book will do you absolutely no good. Each chapter will contain specific psychological exercises or experiments. If you do the exercises, slowly but surely you are going to make contact with your Potential Self and begin to use the psychological powers that now lie dormant within you.

2. Matthew 18:3   3. Luke 10:9

If you read the book and do *not* do the psychological experiments, you will get no more benefit from it than you would get from reading a book on physical fitness and then failing to exercise.

As you are doing these experiments, occasionally your emotions will be stirred. You may feel sad or lonely or overcome with a sudden flood of anger. Or you may experience a great burst of happiness and energy and exhilaration. Although you may not understand what is happening, be reassured that it is quite natural. After all, you are reaching parts of yourself with which you have been out of contact for many years. Connected to these "lost" parts of you are feelings. They may concern something that happened to you at a certain stage of development. Or you may just be filled with emotion at recognizing some old, forgotten part of yourself.

Many people are frightened by their feelings. You have probably also made use of your Repressor in this way: to repress emotions. Part of actualizing your Potential Self is to be able to finally allow yourself to experience *all* of your feelings. Most of them will fade away after you have permitted yourself to experience and accept them.

But if you are so extremely uncomfortable with any of your feelings that it interferes with your progress, then again I suggest you turn to Chapter 10, and consider whether you may want to seek professional help for what is troubling you in your life situation.

My hope in providing for you these exercises and the ones that follow in the rest of the book is that you will consider them an exciting voyage of discovery. In fact, the first exercise *is* a journey.

I am going to suggest that you take a trip backwards through time into your own Inner Space.

Set aside a couple of undisturbed hours. Sit in a comfortable chair or lie on a couch. Imagine you are floating in a warm pool. The water is the same temperature as your body. The air is comfortably warm. You are one with your surroundings and comfortably relaxed. Before you is a TV screen. At first it is blank, but slowly—indistinctly at first and then more clearly—an image appears. It's you. It could be your high school graduation. Your first car. An image of you and your best friend.

A series of random pictures will flash across the screen in quick succession. One picture suggests another. People you haven't thought about in years will appear. You can hardly match their names with their faces. As these pictures come into your mind, they will evoke feelings. Some will be happy memories but others will be of events that were embarrassing or uncomfortable.

As these pictures and feelings emerge, soon you

will be bringing to the surface of your mind what life was like for you as a teen-ager. Stay with those images for awhile.

How were your relationships with your peer group? Did you have close friends or did you tend to be a loner? What did other people think of you? Did you do well in school? Or poorly? What were your feelings about your physical attractiveness? How did you get along with the opposite sex? Were you warm and self-confident and outgoing? Or did you tend to be on the timid and shy side? What were your feelings about sex itself? What kind of sexual relationships did you have, and how did you feel about them? Did you masturbate? Were you able to accept this positively, or did you feel guilty?

What were your relationships with your parents? Did you feel they understood and accepted you? Or did you feel criticized and put down? How did you get along with your brothers or sisters during these years? Were there any persons outside your family who had an important influence on you, such as a teacher, a Scout leader, a minister, or rabbi? In what areas of your personality did you feel "awkward"? What psychological "secrets" about yourself did you keep even from your best friends?

These are some (but not all) of the questions you can ask yourself as you go back in memory to the time of your adolescence. As you reminisce, you will come across negative aspects of your concept of yourself (things you were ashamed of, felt inadequate or guilty about). Do not run away from these things, but deliberately focus on them. Use your technique of negative thinking to purposely exaggerate these negative emotions. Think of specific incidents when you felt negative about yourself.

For example, I remember vividly, over all these years, one particular Saturday when I was fifteen. I called a girl named Ellen to ask her for a date the next weekend. I must have phoned her twelve or fourteen times that day. Each time I got her sister, who told me that Ellen had just gone out or would be back in fifteen minutes or some other excuse. Emotionally blind at the time, I accepted all of this at face value. Finally, around the twelfth or fourteenth call, I heard giggling in the background. And then it dawned on me that I had been had.

Using negative thinking, I could focus on this episode and talk to myself something like this: "You see, Dodson, no girl could possibly be interested in you. You're too tall and skinny. You're not good looking. You have nothing to offer to a girl. No wonder Ellen didn't want to go out with you. Furthermore, you were even too dumb to catch on to what was happening. Ellen and her sister were playing with you like a cat with a mouse. It'll be that way throughout your life. No woman worth her salt is going to want to mess around with you."

You need to emotionally reexperience in this way the important periods of your life, such as the years of adolescence. It's difficult to know precisely what amount of time to use for this, but as a rule of thumb I would suggest you spend a week experiencing each important period of your past. Be sure to spend some time on this every day.

You will be astonished at what will begin flooding into your mind. For example, that incident of my phoning Ellen popped spontaneously into my mind as I was writing this. During your "adolescent week," try to live like an adolescent, think like an adolescent, *be* an adolescent. When you discover any dissatisfaction with your self-concept during those years, use negative thinking on it. You will not enjoy reexperiencing some of these unhappy situations and feelings, but you will be surprised how the technique of negative thinking will buoy you up in spite of it. You will begin to feel less uncomfortable about these old unhappy experiences.

At the end of each week, it is time to answer back to what the voice of negative thinking has been saying.

During the previous week, that voice has been like a prosecuting attorney, painting you in the darkest colors imaginable. Now you need a defense attorney, who will speak favorably for you. For example, on the episode with Ellen, my defense attorney might say: "Your wife loves you very much. She thinks you're handsome and intelligent and that she is lucky to be married to you. You know this because she's told you so. Ellen was a good looking girl when she was fifteen, but she couldn't see beyond the superficial aspects of life. All she could see was a tall, gangly, thin boy that she didn't want to date. Furthermore, she was cruel to make a fool of him. So she did hurt you. What if she didn't find you attractive? Are you going to let her reaction color how you see yourself for the rest of your life? No! Then picture to yourself the boy she didn't see clearly enough to want to date. Inside that tall, gangly, awkward fifteen-year-old boy was an intelligent, interesting, and loving person, who was curious about life in all of its aspects. Ellen missed knowing the Inner You because all she could see was the superficial Outer You. And that inner you is still there. You are still intelligent, interesting, loving, and curious about life. Give yourself credit for these parts of your personality."

This is the sort of thing you need to do. Your defense attorney "talks back" to your prosecuting attorney and points out the solid and good aspects of your personality and character. Take as much time as you need going over your positive points, till you feel you have presented yourself fully and feel good about it.

After exploring adolescence, do the same thing for the next earliest psychological stage, the years from kindergarten or first grade up to age thirteen. As with adolescence, there are many memories which should be readily accessible. How did you like school generally? Was it pleasant and fun or dull and dreary? Did you do well in school and feel adequate about your performance in classes? Or did you do poorly and have a feeling of inadequacy about the academic side of school? Did your parents praise you for your school work, or were they always getting after you? How did you get along with your classmates? Did you have lots of good friends or did you tend to be a loner? Were you good at the sports and competitions of school life, or were you always the last one chosen for the team? Were there any teachers with whom you had especially good relationships? Any teachers you had especially poor relationships with?

What were your relationships with your mother and father during those years? Were they close and happy? Or did you feel that you had to be very guarded about the things you told them or talked over? What sorts of things did your parents praise? What did they scold you for?

Imagine that you are back at some point during those early school years. Of what things are you proud? What things made you feel ashamed? Then use your technique of negative thinking to rid yourself of the negative aspects of your self-image during those years.

For example, the thing that stands out in the negative sense during my preadolescent years was my overprotective mother and her effect on my self-concept. Among the things she would not let me do was learn to swim. She felt that public swimming pools were unclean and germ-ridden, and she wasn't going to expose me to this. Now I can let my negative thinking loose on that scene. "Dodson, the other kids tease you because you aren't allowed to go swimming. Every Saturday in the spring and summer when they go swimming, you have to stay home. It makes you feel awful. You'd give anything if your mother would let you go swimming with the others. It makes you feel different and inadequate because you can't swim. In fact, it proves beyond a shadow of a doubt that you *are* inadequate."

Later, when I give my defense attorney a chance, I say: "Look, you couldn't help it that you had an overprotective mother. So you didn't learn to swim when you were a youngster, and you have never learned to swim to this day. So what? You learned to do many other things. You played basketball, baseball, touch football, tennis, and volleyball. You also learned to draw, cartoon, write, dance well, hike, and backpack. And I want to point out something to you, Dodson. It's true you can't swim, but you never learned to play golf either. Apparently not learning to play golf never bothered you and doesn't now. Why? Because nobody ever teased you about it when you were a little kid. So deliberately torment yourself about swimming for a week, negative practice style, and THEN LET IT GO. Decide that you're not going to think badly about yourself anymore because of something that happened back in grade school."

When we go back beyond kindergarten or first grade to the first five years of life, very few of us can remember much about this period. Here I suggest you let your mind rove free and find as many

incidents as you can remember. Most people are
able to remember only four or five. Whatever these
early memories are, think of them as plays. You
play all the parts and see what you may learn about
yourself.

For example, here is the earliest memory of a
patient of mine. His mother was at the hospital
having his baby brother. He, a five-year-old, was
at home. He remembers trying to ride his tricycle
down the steep front steps of his house and hurt-
ing himself. As I had him recall this memory and
express his feelings out loud this is what came out:
"I'm riding this dumb tricycle down these steep
steps. This is a stupid thing to do because I'll probably get myself hurt. Ooops! There it goes—
owwww—that hurt a lot! That'll make my mother
pay attention! I don't know what she's doing at
that darn hospital, but if I hurt myself, then she'll
have to come home and pay attention to me!" This
gave my patient new insight about how he continually caused bad things to happen to himself
so that someone important would pay attention.

Try to focus especially on the earliest memory
you have of your mother. Then the earliest memory of your father. See if these scenes throw any
light on your concept of yourself. Were these early
memories of your mother and father happy or un-

happy? Was the role you played in the memory a strong and confident one or a weak one?

Finally, we want to get back in imagination to the preverbal state, before you were old enough to talk and conceptualize. I suggest a simple technique which some of you may feel is absurd. Go ahead and try it even though it may seem ludicrous. You should do this when nobody else is around to see or hear you. Lie on the floor. Curl up in the fetal position, which is a most primitive posture and one of great helplessness. First, cry out "Mommy" or "Help, Mommy" for about twenty-five times in a row. Just use those words and no others, repeating them louder and louder each time. See what memories or feelings come flowing into your mind. Then do the same by calling out "Daddy" or "Help, Daddy." If negative thoughts or feelings emerge from this exercise, use negative thinking to get rid of them. If positive thoughts or feelings emerge, welcome them.

Now, let's take stock. How far have you come? What have you done? You have taken four or five weeks and gone back over your life. You began with adolescence and traced down negative aspects of your self-concept which have been built into the way you think about yourself today. You have freely expressed these negative aspects and freely responded with the positive ones. Now, having gone backwards in time, you are going to reverse yourself and go forwards.

Here you are going to give your powerful psychological imagination a chance to work for you instead of against you. You are going to imagine that you are, quite literally, born again. Begin with the good parts, the warm and loving aspects of your parents' personalities, and imagine that they are relating to you with only those loving feelings.

Then picture the negative and unloving parts of your parents' personalities. Try to imagine what your parents must have been like as children. Underneath each negative facet of their personalities is a hurt, miserable, and angry little child. Try to see how the way your parents were hurt and psychologically wounded when they were children is what caused them to be harsh and unloving with you. See if this enables you to forgive your parents for the negative things they have done to you. Some of you may find this hard to do, some easy. Do the best you can.

Do the same thing with your brothers or sisters. Rejoice in the loving parts of their personalities. Try to understand and forgive the unloving parts. This psychological "meeting" with members of your family may arouse deep feelings in you. Try to experience the feelings freely. Let them flow through you and then fade away in their own time.

Next, bring yourself up to the school years. Concentrate on the positive parts of your personality first, the parts that did well in class or were adequate in sports or well-liked by peers. Then hold an imaginary ceremony: drop into a trash can those parts of yourself which were not adequate or which you did not like. Now use your imagination to endow yourself with positive traits to replace the negative parts you have consigned to the junk heap. Imagine yourself being treated differently by your friends, your parents, or your teachers during these school years.

Do the same for adolescence. In particular, imagine yourself having a dialogue with your parents in which you tell them hidden things about yourself. Imagine them accepting these revelations and in turn revealing to you hidden secrets from their own adolescence which you never knew about.

How much time will this unique personality journey take, as you are psychologically "born again," beginning with your cries for help from a fetal position on the floor and taking yourself up to yesterday? I do not know. Any suggestion would be purely arbitrary. Take as long as you need.

144

Remember that your goal in doing all of this is to have positive, warm, and confident feelings about yourself. You want to eliminate, as far as possible, any negative and inadequate feelings that you acquired in childhood. This doesn't mean that you are going to have a 100 percent positive self-concept after this experience. From time to time you may need to rework particularly difficult periods.

The psychological experience of being "born again" and systematically undoing the psychological scars and wounds from the various stages of your past life could be the most valuable time you ever spent.

You'll never know until you try.

7: Making Friends With The Creative Child Within You

The previous chapter described how you needed to be born again psychologically in order to relate to your Potential Self. As you went through the rebirth process, you came to realize how you were molded and influenced by outside forces: your parents, relatives, teachers, and friends. They may not have meant to, but they changed you from an outgoing, zestful toddler to a constrained adult hobbled by your Repressive Self. You will confront your Repressive Self not once but many times during your journey through life. Constantly you will have to battle this force, for it prevents you from becoming the real you—*the you that could be.*

In this chapter I want to help you uncover those creative forces which were active within you when you were an uninhibited toddler.

When you were a toddler, about a year old, you were unafraid to try new things and to express your feelings. The world was truly a fascinating place. You had an endless curiosity and a virtual love affair with life. If you were lucky, your parents allowed you to explore your exciting toddler's world. Many children were not so lucky. Their parents slapped their hands or said "No-no, don't touch that" and a thousand other similar things. Much of your zest and self-confidence in exploring the world have been stifled by parents, schools, and other repressive agents of society.

But that uninhibited, zesty, self-confident toddler still lives within you. The problem is how to get in touch with him or her. How can you give your inner creative self a chance? One of the best ways is to use nonverbal activities such as music, dance, and art. Why? Because these activities tend to bypass your defense mechanisms in ways that purely verbal approaches such as thinking and talking do not.

Start with rhythm. This is probably the most primitive nonverbal activity you can use. Our cavemen ancestors made rhythm by beating two sticks together or hitting a rock with a stick. It is also primitive in your own childhood history, whether you consciously remember it or not. You banged "something" with "something" to make your own early childhood rhythms.

I suggest you get something you can bang on with a stick. It can be a tin can or a tin pan of any size. It can be a can with a rock or pebbles inside it. Or an old pie plate. Or a cigar box. Or a bottle. The "stick" can be a drumstick or a branch from a tree. Or an old spoon.

Use your stick and your "something" and start beating out a rhythm. Be very loose and experimental. Try different rhythms and approaches; don't get fixated on one. Then try it faster. Or slower. Music at this point is unnecessary; don't even hum a tune. You are creating your own rhythms—from your body, from your own feelings.

Do this alone. It's inhibiting to have anybody else around when you want to let yourself go.

After you have been using homemade instruments for a while, you may want to move on to something different. For example, you may want to invest in some inexpensive bongo drums. Let your fingers feel the vibrations they make as they tap or bang the bongos. You can experiment with all kinds or combinations of rhythms. For variety, try a tambourine.

After you feel at ease in producing different rhythms, allow fantasies to come into your mind as you play. I will avoid any specific example, because I want them to be your own unique fantasies. I will comment, however, that people who have performed these drumming exercises, often experience sexual fantasies. Whatever images form in your mind, don't block them out. Go with them and imagine the fantasies are actually happening.

If you find this is hard for you or you think to yourself, "What's a grown-up like me doing fooling around with this kid stuff?", then immediately stop the exercise. Use negative thinking to lecture yourself, deliberately exaggerating how foolish you feel banging on drums and having fantasies. Take the role of a parental figure and criticize yourself severely. Say such things as "Come on now, you're sales manager of your company; this is ridiculous for you to be making a fool of yourself with these kid games and tomfoolery." Then after you have finished using the negative thinking technique, resume the rhythmic exercise and see how you feel about it.

It is impossible to suggest how many days or weeks you should spend on each exercise. Do what feels good. If you find yourself getting bored with what you are doing, it's time to move on to something else.

When you feel completely comfortable doing the rhythmic exercises, you are ready to move on to dancing. Some people are really uptight about dancing. They may have never learned at all. Or they may dance in a very inhibited, subdued manner. Outwardly they appear natural, but inside they feel uncomfortable. If you are one of those people, have no fear. The kind of dancing I'm talking about is nothing like ballroom dancing.

What I have in mind is the "dancing" a very young child will do. Continue the rhythms you have become familiar with, only this time move around the room. If you feel inhibited, then stand in place but move your head or sway your shoulders or torso. Pretty soon your feet are bound to follow. Your goal is to move around the room, letting your body express the rhythm you're tapping out. When you feel comfortable doing this, speed up the rhythm in drumming and dancing. Then try the reverse and go very slowly.

After you feel at ease with many different rates of drumming and dancing, let fantasies come into your mind as you dance. For a painfully shy person, this could be particularly helpful, since what shy people dread the most is to be the center of attraction. If this is part of the problem of your Repressive Self, here is an excellent opportunity to lick it.

In my clinical practice I have found that shy people not only dread being the center of attention because they are being noticed but because they are afraid of being sexually attractive. If this is part of your problem, explore it in your fantasies. As you dance, imagine you are the center of a circle of admirers. Confront your Repressive Self. Tell it that you *are* an attractive person and that there is nothing wrong with being appreciated.

Up till now you have been using rhythms which came entirely from inside you. I did not want you to use records, tapes, or the radio because you should not be worried, consciously or unconsciously, whether your rhythm or dancing "matched" what you were hearing. We wanted to concentrate only on your own internal rhythms.

Now it is time to go to a music store and browse around for records or tapes which you can use to interpret your own creativity. You can drum along or dance to these records. And again, by dancing, I mean the free-form movements of your own body following where the music leads, rather than following a set pattern of steps.

When you pick out records or tapes, start with the kind of music that makes you feel comfortable. It may be rock, classical, or the drum music of a primitive culture. Even though you begin with the music with which you feel most at ease, experiment with many other kinds of less familiar music as well. Always let the music "flow through" you and let your body move in whatever way it wants. Imagine that you are a very young child, hearing the music for the first time and responding to it.

Here are some types of music you could try, in your own order of preference: any kind of rock music, primitive drum music, such as that of Africa or Tahiti; music from foreign lands, such as that of Bali, Greece, Mexico; classical music of all varieties; jazz music of many styles. You may have initial negative reactions to some of these suggestions. I urge you to give all of them at least one try. You may find, for example, by trying music you have an initial negative reaction to, that it brings out fearful feelings in you, and that is what is behind your negative reaction. This music gives you a chance to face that fear and conquer it.

As you dance to all of these different kinds of music, you should be alone. Don't let someone else's presence inhibit you. And now it's time to let your fantasies run riot! Imagine that people are viewing you as you dance. You are the center of many admiring eyes. See how your fantasies change as you shift from dancing to music like Debussy's "La Mer" to Tahitian drums to Dixieland.

Next we come to art. At this point I can hear some of you saying, "Now hold on. I can bang a can with a stick, I can dance around a room, but I'm no artist. You're out of my league now!" Others of you may be mumbling, "I can't even draw a straight line." Let me remind you again of the purpose of these nonverbal exercises. I'm not trying to teach you to become an accomplished musician, dancer, or artist. I'm trying to help you free the creative child within you. You don't have to become an "artist" in the strict sense you are thinking about. What I want is to help you go back in time and express yourself in art the way you would have when you were a very young child.

Go to an art store and pick up a large brush (not a tiny one) and a large pad of inexpensive, unused newsprint. Or you can use old newspaper itself. After all, there's no reason why you can't paint right over printing.

Paints fall into two categories: those that are not water-soluble and those that are. The ones that are not water-soluble are the oil paints. You need turpentine for thinning these, and they are fairly complicated for beginners. I suggest you concentrate on the water-soluble paints: water colors, tempera, and acrylics. Water colors are the thinnest. You cannot cover a darker color with a lighter one as you can with the acrylics. There is no reason why these media cannot be combined, and you may want to try all of them.

Once you have gathered your materials, you are ready to begin. Imagine you are a two-year-old and that you are *not* trying to paint a specific picture of anything. You are just experimenting with colors to see how they look together. (If you can arrange it, visit a nursery school to see how young children actually paint or color.) One easy way to begin is to dip your brush in clear water and cover the paper with it until it is all wet. Then dip your brush into a color and put it on the paper. Now try another color. Or try painting on dry paper. See how different the effects are.

Spend plenty of time just painting colors on paper. Or squiggling lines on paper. But in no way should you attempt to draw something that looks like anything.

Sometimes it's fun to paint to music. Take one of the records you danced to and paint to it. Just as you previously let the music dictate your body movements, now let it dictate the way the paint flows.

You may want to try crayons as well as paints. I suggest oil pastel crayons instead of the usual wax crayons, because the colors are far more vivid and striking.

As you experiment with paints and crayons, see what feelings are stirred inside you by the different colors. And see how you feel as you mix them.

After you begin to feel comfortable using paints or crayons, it's time to move one step further. There is an art technique which can combine the use of both your conscious and unconscious mind. And I think it will do it in a way that will not arouse inhibitions in you and have you saying to yourself, "But what I draw doesn't look like a horse!" Here is how it works. Begin by drawing fantasy animals. The advantage of doing this is that since the animal is fantasy anyway, how can you possibly worry whether it looks like a horse or a dog or an anteater?

First of all, close your eyes. Imagine some kind of animal. Try to picture it very clearly in your mind: its color, size, and general outline. Then open your eyes and make a mark on the paper. That is where you are going to begin. It can be the top of the animal's head, the tip of its tail, or the left toenail on its right front paw. It doesn't matter. All that matters is that is where you are going to start.

Let's say you decide to start with the head. Put your pencil or crayon on the paper where the head will be. Then close your eyes and imagine how the head of your fantasy animal looks. Draw as much of the head as feels comfortable to you. Then stop, and open your eyes.

Check your progress and see where you are in your drawing. Then put your pencil where you left off, close your eyes again, and draw the rest of the head.

Continue this eyes open/eyes closed method until the whole drawing is completed.

The formula you are using is this: when your

eyes are open, you are using your conscious mind. When your eyes are closed, you are using your unconscious mind. This will help you to be more uninhibited about your drawing, since you obviously cannot control the lines you draw when your eyes are closed. Naturally you will draw with less inhibition, more daring and better imagination than if your eyes were open all the time.

After you have drawn your fantasy animal, you may want to draw a fantasy background: trees, shrubs, a sun or moon, all using the same eyes open/eyes closed technique.

Color in your fantasy animal and background, and once again see what fantasies or feelings it arouses in you.

Draw a number of different fantasy animals this way. When you feel comfortable with this technique, draw a picture of your mother. And your father. Don't rush through this. Take your time and see what fantasies and feelings come to mind about each of them. If you had brothers or sisters, draw them.

Next, draw a picture of your present family, if you are married. Finally, draw a picture of yourself. Take time to explore all of the fantasies and feelings brought to mind by your drawing of yourself. Then, since no one is 100 percent masculine or 100 percent feminine, draw a picture of yourself as if you were the opposite sex. Once again, explore your fantasies about this.

If you have carried out all of these psychological experiments over a period of weeks, you will have made contact with a whole new world of feelings and thoughts. Your defense mechanisms have been inhibiting you for years when it comes to verbal activities such as thinking or talking. But they have not had much practice inhibiting you in activities such as rhythm, dance, or art.

When you venture into these nonverbal areas, you are bound to make contact, at an unconscious level, with the creative young child within you. You will surely become a freer, more feeling person, as you experiment with the parts of yourself that you have neglected for years.

Having experimented with nonverbal, you are finally ready for the verbal. A nineteenth century Scandinavian writer once wrote an essay called, "How to Become an Original Writer in Three Days." This is what he suggested. Set aside twenty or thirty minutes the first day and write down every single thought that comes into your mind. Do not censor yourself in any way, such as "That's unimportant; no sense writing that down," or "That's an ugly or sadistic thought; I won't write that." Write down *everything*. Do the same thing the second day and the third. If you have been perfectly honest, you will have plenty of material to start you on a career as an original writer.

I want to adapt this suggestion somewhat. You may want to write by hand, type, or talk into a tape recorder. All of these are okay. But be sure you are by yourself so that you do not censor yourself in the slightest. If you do this in utter honesty, you will probably be amazed at the thoughts or feelings that come out of you.

You see, what you are really doing during that twenty or thirty minutes is *listening to the voice of yourself.* Until you try an experiment such as this, you are not aware that you spend your days listening only to the voices of other people. The other people may be friends, coworkers, bosses, or teachers. The voices may be written down in newspapers, magazines, or books, or appear in electronic form through radio or TV. Nevertheless, they are *other* people's voices, *other* people's ideas, and *other* people's opinions. Very few people take the time to listen to the uncensored voice of themselves.

If you do nothing more than take these twenty or thirty minutes every day and listen to your own uncensored voice, I can think of no more powerful thing you can do to get in touch with your Potential Self. This one exercise could literally change your life!

Let me give you an example of how this exercise practically saved a patient's business as well as his personality from going down the tubes. When I first met Lou, he was an extremely successful real estate broker. He had drifted into real estate after unsuccessfully trying accounting, and somehow he just clicked once he got into sales. He was so good that after a year of working for someone else, he opened up his own firm and ten months later had three branch offices.

But he had to work long and tiring hours to achieve his success. His wife was very unhappy that she saw so little of him, and his compulsive work was threatening to break up his marriage. When he came to me for therapy, we had great success in helping him find the creative child within him and in learning to work more playfully, zestfully, and less compulsively. Once he understood his drives and the reasons behind them, he was able to pace himself better and he no longer needed therapy.

I was somewhat surprised when, almost two years later, he called and made an appointment. The real estate market was in a bad slump, he told me. Interest rates were so high that no one was buying unless they absolutely had to. To make matters worse, the aircraft and electronics industries which employed many of the area's residents were having massive layoffs. People were leaving to take jobs elsewhere if they could find them. Real estate offices were folding right and left. Lou had to close his least productive branch. It bothered him to have to put people out of work. And he was afraid he might be forced to go out of business himself.

He felt he needed to think of some new and clever ways of promoting his business. There had to be some way to make potential buyers come to him, he reasoned. He kept trying to figure out some special way to bring in business, but he couldn't. It soon got to be a vicious circle. The harder he tried to think of a gimmick, the more it escaped him. And the more it escaped him, the more desperate he became. The more desperate he became, the less he could think.

He became despondent. He couldn't even do a normal day's work. Some days, instead of going to the office, he would drive his car to the cliffs overlooking the ocean and sit there all morning, obsessively brooding. "What's the use?" he would ask his wife. "It's beginning to look like it doesn't make any difference whether I'm there in the office or not. That's a hell of a thing for the president of a company to have to admit!" Finally he was feeling so depressed and unhappy that he phoned me for an appointment.

The first thing we agreed on was that he would never get any good ideas for his business in his present state of tension. He would have to break through that self-destructive pattern. We remembered his past success with the creative child exercises, and decided to try them again.

I suggested that he take his family for a long weekend and get away completely from the old environment of office and home. At first he protested, reminding me that real estate was busiest on weekends, and he was needed in the office then. It was only when I pointed out that being at the office was doing him harm, and that he absolutely *had* to get away, that he finally agreed to go, although very reluctantly. He decided to take the family and go to Palm Springs, about two hours' drive away.

He rented an apartment with a pool for four days. His wife took along some books, the kids took their bikes, and everybody took their bathing suits. I suggested he bring along a lot of crayons, a number of pads of unused newsprint, and a tape recorder.

I told him that he had been using only what I call the "thinking of the right hand," which is governed by the conscious mind and is orderly, logical, and rational, proceeding step by step to logical conclusions. But he had not yet been using the "thinking of the left hand," which is intuitive, hunchy, governed by the unconscious mind, and is responsible for new discoveries in science or breakthroughs in the field of business. I told him that the key to using the thinking of the left hand was to get in touch with the creative child within him. Working together, we devised a four-day plan for contacting his creative inner child.

I told him to get the others out of the apartment, and sit by himself at the kitchen table or in the living room simply scribbling, doodling, or drawing. As much as he could, he was to get into the role of a child, and feel like a child, not a grown-up, sitting there scribbling and doodling. If any words popped into his mind, he was to print the word on a pad and then let his mind wander freely over the word, talking into his tape recorder as he did so.

What I was counting on was this. Because of his previous hard work and the enormous amount of thinking he had done about his business, he had accumulated plenty of raw material in his brain related to his business. All we had to do was to help him loosen up, get in touch with that playful, creative little child within himself, and he would be able to put the raw material together in the form of new ideas.

I told Lou that if he did get any new ideas on how to improve his business, he should simply jot the idea down on small note paper, but not attempt to think about it or elaborate on it at that time. Most of the time he was to confine himself to being like a child, scribbling, doodling, and fooling around with colors. He spent most of Saturday doing this. Then he went for a swim, ate an early dinner, took a long walk, and slept the night through for the first time in a month.

On Sunday the rest of the family again went their separate ways. Lou went back to his attempts to contact the creative child within him. At first nothing special happened. He was doodling and scribbling as he had the day before. Then words began to pop into his mind, and he would print the word on his pad and doodle around it. Then he would free-associate to the word with his tape recorder. At first the going was slow, but then it suddenly seemed as if his mental dam had burst. Ideas began to come flooding forth. As the ideas came, he jotted them down. Not all of them were usable. Some were too far-out and impractical. But others proved to be just what he had been looking for unsuccessfully for weeks.

One of the ideas he got was a new and catchy motto he could use on all of the promotion pieces for his business. That idea alone was worth its weight in gold, because once a person heard this motto, it was hard to forget it, and whenever he thought of the motto, he would identify it with Lou's real estate firm.

Another idea that came to him was this. He had been reading about the "feedback technique" of dealing with children's feelings in one of my books on child raising. Suddenly the idea popped in his mind: if this technique works in helping children to know that adults understand their feelings, why wouldn't it work to help customers know that real estate salesmen truly understand their feelings about high interest rates and their frustrations about the financial difficulties of buying a house? So he decided to teach his salesmen this technique to use in dealing with customers.

After the outpouring of ideas Saturday afternoon, Lou felt drained. He decided to take the next two days to just laze around and do nothing. Even so, a few more ideas came to him on Monday and Tuesday, and he jotted them down.

The new ideas and the new feelings of hope and enthusiasm for his work helped tide Lou over the difficult business period. Then, when times got better, he was able to use some of the other ideas he had produced during the Palm Springs weekend to further expand his business. Today he is president of one of the most thriving real estate firms in the area. He must have ten or twelve branch offices now, and just recently he opened a new real estate school. He was so pleased with what he jokingly calls the "nursery school" method of getting new ideas that he has used it often in his business. He has even taught it to some of the key people in his firm.

I ran into him in a department store about six months ago and began joshing him about his terrific business success. "Lou," I said, "how come your firm is so far ahead of all the other real estate companies in our area?"

"Because," he said with a wink, "we're the only real estate firm in the South Bay that knows how to think with our left hand, and we're the only firm that employs a creative child as a business consultant!"

As a matter of fact, not only do I teach this technique to patients such as Lou, but I use this same technique myself.

During the year that it took me to write my first book on child raising, I kept trying to think of a title. Writing the book was easy compared to coming up with a title for it. It seems to me that I thought of and discarded literally thousands of possible titles. Things like *A Mother's Guide to Her Child's Earlyhood*, and *Scientific Secrets of Child Raising*, and *Those All-Important First Five Years*. Nothing sounded right. After about eight or nine months I was feeling more and more frustrated.

Then the obvious thought hit me between the eyes. "Hey, Dodson," I said to myself, "you've been teaching your patients for years to use childlike thinking to stimulate the 'thinking of the left hand.' Why don't you use it yourself?"

So I did. I took the family away on a weekend camping trip. The rest of the family "did their own thing" while I retired down a tree-covered canyon with several newsprint tablets and a batch of crayons. Just like Lou, I scribbled and doodled and did all the other things I've talked about to try to contact the creative child within me. I worked hard at the creative child exercises on Saturday, and then on Sunday I didn't do anything in particular, except laze around the forest and stream. And sure enough, as I was driving home in the camper on Sunday night, the title *How to Parent* popped into my mind. A problem that nine months of adult thinking had failed to deal with had been solved in two days by using creative child exercises!

These are only two of many examples I could give to show you how valuable it can be for you to learn to get in touch with your inner creative child. Once you and that child were quite literally one and the same person. Now the child is hidden within your adult facade. These exercises will help you get back in touch with him or her.

Of course, these exercises take a lot of time. But look at how much time you're already spending in promoting your Repressive Self. Although the shift from Repressor to Potential Self does take extra time, your main energies will soon be directed toward developing your own potential. You'll find you don't have time left for the old repressive ways. Once you start to get in touch with your inner child's colorful, zesty, uninhibited, self-confident approach to life, you will never be the same again!

8: From the "You" of Today To the "You" of Tomorrow

Many people are eager to get from the "you" of today to the "you" that could be: your Potential Self. They are aware that their present selves are full of inadequacies and weaknesses. They want to be free from the old "you" and become an assertive and self-confident "you," capable of handling all situations.

Unfortunately, many people think the way to do this is to cover up today's weak self so that they can gradually arrive at a strong and self-confident self. But they are proceeding the wrong way, as a case from my clinical practice illustrates.

I refer to a thirty-two-year-old, newly divorced man. Call him Harry. He suddenly found himself trying to cope with dating and meeting new women after nine years of marriage. He went to singles dances, but he was terrified to ask a girl to dance. Sometimes he would spend the whole evening in the bar, drinking and talking with some of the other men. He did not have the courage to ask a girl to dance, which was the reason he had come there in the first place. On occasions, he would manage to ask several girls to dance but then not be able to talk much about anything, because he was nervous.

He handled this particular problem in a manner typical of most people who have uncomfortable feelings they are ashamed of. His unconscious motto was: "Try to keep other people from finding out how you really feel inside. Cover up your feelings of weakness and fear. Appear poised and collected."

I suggested that he handle the situation differently. First I directed him to use negative thinking in my office, as he role-played the situation. I had him deliberately exaggerate his fears and say to himself, "If she only knew how scared I am inside, she would despise me. What girl wants to dance with a guy who's so neurotic he's scared to ask her? Anyway, if she really knew what I'm like, she wouldn't have anything more to do with me.

170

So I have to fool her into thinking I'm a cool guy who really knows his way around or I'm sunk."

After he had tried negative thinking in role-playing, I suggested that the next dance he attended he should try an entirely different approach. He should pick a girl he wanted to dance with and ask her. But instead of trying to impress her, he should have the courage to be his real self, the "you" he was now. He should tell her how scared he was to ask her to dance. It took some persuasion to get him to do this, because he was convinced that such an approach spelled psychological disaster. Nevertheless, he finally agreed to try it.

Can you guess the girl's response? Did she spurn and ridicule him for being "weak" and scared? Far from it! She said, "I'm really glad you told me that, because a girl friend talked me into coming here, and I was afraid no one would ask me to dance!" Far from having nothing to talk about, he found that he and the girl talked for a long time about their fearful feelings of coping with the new and frightening world of divorce. He made the same kind of revelation to other girls at the dance, with the same general results. And he wound up getting dates with several of them.

He was amazed when he came in for his therapy hour the next week. "Doc, I thought you were crazy when you told me to do that, but it really works!" I underlined for him why it "really works." When we try to hide our real feelings from other people, we are constantly afraid they will find out. We are like spies in an enemy country, always afraid a gesture or an accent will give us away.

But when we have the courage to present the "you" that we really are at the present moment, feelings of weakness and all, then four (and probably more) very important things happen. First, it requires courage to tell other people our feelings of weakness, so we are learning to be more courageous. Second, when we confront our feelings of weakness, we are also learning to be less afraid of them, and they begin to lose their hold over us. Third, instead of other people despising us when they learn of our fears and weaknesses (which is what we fantasize will happen), people actually like us better for exposing these feelings. Why? Because we are more human when we dare to admit our imperfections, which helps other people to accept their own insecure feelings. Fourth, we are giving the other person a good feeling about our honesty and openness. More important, we are relieving ourselves of the burden of being deceptive, so that we can relax and have a good time.

Each of these things is self-reinforcing and leads us to repeat the same good experience again later.

Let me tell you about my own experience in this area. Years ago, when I first started my public speaking career, I was so nervous that I typed out everything I was going to say and read directly from the manuscript. In time I felt relaxed enough to speak from notes. Finally I got to the point where I felt confident enough to speak without notes at all.

Speaking without notes has several advantages. It gives you tremendous eye contact with your audience. It enables you to take advantage of spontaneous incidents or laughter that arise in the course of the speech. You can comment in a way that is impossible with a "canned" lecture.

However, speaking without notes has one great danger. What if you can't remember what comes next? You have nothing on the lectern to refresh your memory. For several years, during speaking engagements, I lived with the fear that my mind would go blank and that I simply wouldn't be able to remember part of my speech.

Well, it finally happened. I was giving the third of a four-lecture series. This particular lecture had three main points. While finishing up point one, I suddenly became aware that I couldn't for the life of me remember point two. I stalled. I embellished point one, hoping desperately I would remember point two. But it was no use. Finally I turned to the audience and said, "I may as well confess something. My mind has gone blank and I can't remember point two. I will have to skip it and go on to point three. I know that isn't going to make a great deal of sense to you, but it's the best I can do in the situation."

I went on to point three, and after talking for five or six minutes, point two suddenly popped into my mind. Immediately I stopped and said, "I just remembered point two so I'll go back to that now, and then I will finish up with point three." Of course I was mortified. But I was amazed at the people's response to that lecture. Of all four lectures in the series, a written evaluation indicated that the audiences liked that one best! In addition, an enormous number of people came up to me after the lecture and said something like this: "That was great the way you handled that situation—you were so human!" One man said, "I could see myself up there, forgetting what I was supposed to say next."

That experience taught me many valuable lessons. It taught me that people rarely "put you down" when you have the courage to level with them about your weakness. And, incidentally, I have never had my mind go blank in a lecture again! I suspect the reason is that I am no longer afraid of this happening. I know how to handle it if it should ever happen, so I have nothing to be afraid of.

There are some dangers I want to warn you about in connection with this sharing of the "weak" side of your personality. First, it is not wise to point out your weaknesses to someone who is in a position of power over you. It can be used against you by your boss, for example, unless you know for sure that he is a most unusual and understanding person. If you are a salesman, it is hardly wise to confide in your sales manager, "You know, when I go to call on a prospect, I'm often so nervous I feel like throwing up!"

Let's analyze why it is a mistake to tell certain people these kinds of feelings. Everybody has feelings of weakness, whether they admit it or not. When you tell someone your feelings of fear and inadequacy, you stimulate his own feelings of weakness. If he shares his feelings with you as you did with him, then the two of you move closer emotionally. This is exactly what happened with my patient at the dance.

But the exact opposite outcome is possible. There are people who are very uptight about admitting to any fears or feelings of inadequacy. They can only picture themselves as strong in every way. For example, I have dealt with people in my clinical practice who have said, "I hate to be so weak that I have to come and tell you my troubles. I should be able to handle my problems myself." When you reveal your feelings of weakness to an uptight person and arouse in him an awareness of the things he feels insecure about, you scare him. His defense against this is often to denounce your weakness and to put you down. If, in addition, he is your boss, you particularly don't want that to happen. So choose carefully who you reveal your weaknesses to.

Second, do not reveal your weakness as a ploy to try to get sympathy. It will have the opposite effect. People will soon think of you as "That oaf who is always telling other people his problems." The revealing of your weakness must not be a total way of life, but a specific response to a specific problem, such as Harry's fears at the dance, or my mind going blank in the midst of a speech.

Third, don't expect an equal amount of openness from others. People will vary from very closed to very open with respect to their ability to share their feelings. Even if the other person is not sadistic or is not trying to put you down, your openness may be more than he can take at the moment. He may give you various signs such as changing the subject, or moving slightly away from you. These nonverbal signs mean that you have become more open about sharing these feelings than he is able to handle. Respect the cues he is giving you and back off.

With those warnings about being too indiscriminate, let's get back to the main point. In twenty years of clinical practice, almost every person who has consulted me has at some time in the course of his therapy said: "You know, I've never told anyone about this before." I have observed that they always feel better after they tell me what they have been hiding for so many years. As long as it was hidden and secret, their weakness or psychological secret was never *accepted* by another human being. But after they tell me, they feel it *is* accepted, and it somehow then loses its psychological hold over them.

This then generates the exercise that goes with this chapter. I suggest that once a week you think of something you have never told anybody. Make the time dimension specific (once a week) or your fears will prevent you from doing it at all.

Next, think of some person you like, who you are used to talking to. Arrange to see that person where you can be alone. After a few minutes of conversation, say: "May I confide something to you that I've never told anybody before? It's not easy for me to do this." You must realize that you are taking a certain risk (of the kinds we mentioned) in being this open. And, of course, there are certain things it is wisest not to disclose. For example, if you have ever served time in jail, it may be better not to tell that!

Be prepared for a spontaneous confiding of feelings on the part of the other person. When you begin to share feelings of inadequacy, hurt, loneliness, you will be amazed sometimes how your "confession" will open the floodgates of emotion in another person.

But also be prepared if the other person simply cannot empathize or accept your feelings of weakness. When you say, "I felt so nervous at that meeting; my stomach was really churning," he may respond, "How can you say something like that? I thought it was a terrific meeting." Take your cue and do not confide any other feelings of weakness to that person.

When you try out the little experiments in this chapter, you are really swimming upstream and against the psychological currents of American life. For we Americans know each other very superficially. Members of my therapy groups comment from time to time, "You know, I could never let my hair down and talk to people outside the way I talk here." That is a shame. They should be able to talk openly about your feelings with some individuals outside the group as well as with the people in the group.

When you start opening yourself up and exposing the real "you" with both strengths and weaknesses, you are going against the typical superficial contact which most Americans make with each other. On the one hand, you may scare people; on the other, they may be deeply thankful that you have opened up and given them the courage to open up to you.

When we confide feelings of weakness to another person, we gain strength. By showing feelings of weakness, we learn courage. That's what it does for us every time, regardless of whether the other person responds with openness or not.

One of the important things we gradually learn is this: The "you" of today is made up of strengths and weaknesses. We fear to share the weakness with others, for we are afraid they could not accept us if they knew we harbored such feelings. So we look forward to the "you" of tomorrow, which we naively expect will be composed only of strengths. We create this illusionary "you"—although we are very much aware of how *we* feel inside—because we don't know how other people feel inside. Looking at them only externally, we imagine they have no feelings of fear, nervousness, hurt, or loneliness. This harks back to ourselves as little children when we saw our parents as all-powerful and all-sufficient giants without any feelings of fear, doubt, or inadequacy.

I remember one patient, a forty-year-old businessman named Norman. He suffered agonies when seated around the conference table with his co-workers thrashing out business problems. He felt nervous and inadequate. He said things to me like, "Here I am nervous as a cat, with my stomach turning over, and those other guys at the office are calm and confident." I pointed out to him that he had no way of knowing how the other fellows felt inside, anymore than they had of knowing his inner feelings. Eventually I encouraged him to talk to the person in the group he felt most secure with and tell him his feelings. To Norman's utter amazement, the other fellow confessed that he also felt nervous and jittery at the meetings, and that he blamed it on the way the president of the company conducted the meetings. Once he had found out how the other fellow felt, Norman's self-concept took a giant step forward.

Nearly everybody has a "you" of tomorrow that they would like to become. Most of these people are pursuing an illusion. For the "you" of tomorrow will not consist only of strengths and self-confidence. It will also consist of weaknesses and feelings of fear and inadequacy. But by finding other people with whom you can share your feelings of weakness, inadequacy, fear, loneliness, and of hurt, you will find that these feelings lose their power over you. No longer are they shameful secrets you must keep inside. For you have found that you can share them and have them accepted.

9. Programming Yourself For Success

In this chapter I want to talk about your goals and plans and how you can program yourself for success. Your Potential Self thrives on well-made goals that reflect what is important to you.

A goal is an objective you want to achieve. A plan is a specific way of reaching that goal. Both goals and plans are *ideas in your mind*.

Look around you. Everything you see in the world around you (unless it is a part of nature) began as an idea in somebody's mind. The suit or dress you are wearing. The car you drive. The music you listen to.

This book you are reading began as an idea in

my mind. Then the idea became a goal, and I created a plan to achieve it. The typewriter I wrote it on was originally the idea of an eighteenth-century Englishman named Henry Mill. It has been continuously developed and refined by a series of other people since and represents an achieved goal for each of them. Everything you wear, everything in your house or apartment, even the building itself had to be thought of before it could exist. And then the design, manufacturing, and marketing of it became goals for someone. Even your toothbrush began as an idea, with a specific plan to achieve it.

All tangible objects began as goals, plans, or ideas in the minds of people. This is a revolutionary concept, once you really allow it to grasp you, for it brings home the importance of the world of thought. Unfortunately, many Americans tend to downgrade the world of thought. When we call a person an intellectual, it is not always meant as a compliment. We respect the people who are characterized as "doers," forgetting that every "doer" is first a thinker. Looking at things in this incomplete manner prevents us from seeing clearly that *the world is changed by goals and plans conceived in the minds of men and women.*

It is really incredible when you realize that our

school system consistently neglects to teach students how to set their own goals and make realistic plans to achieve them. Did you ever hear of a course like that in high school? In college? I never have.

Frequently our schools even neglect to call attention to the fact that such vital activities exist. The thought of setting goals and making plans just "escapes the mind" of many people. And yet, few things are more important to a person in achieving success in all fields of life than learning how to do it. This idea should really exist as a way of life and should be passed on from parents to their children.

I sometimes mention goals and plans to people and ask them what it brings to mind. Most people say: "Oh, success in the business world, in science, or something like that." They usually don't mention the nonprofessional, personal world, such as their marriage.

I think of a former patient of mine, Arthur, a forty-three-year-old man who owned his business and came to me because of increasing "attacks of nerves," as he put it, in his work. He had just opened his second men's clothing store. Business was doing well financially, but his problems with the manager of his newly opened store were increasing. The manager had been a most satisfactory employee until he assumed his new position. Now suddenly he wanted to change many of the concepts that had brought success to Arthur in the first place. Having always prided himself on his business judgment, Arthur was now losing confidence in himself. Was he falling behind the times? At forty-three, was he becoming an old fogy?

As he discussed his business problems, Arthur kept mentioning his wife, Marie. They had been married for twenty years and had two teen-age children. He often remarked how supportive and helpful his wife had been in the beginning when he had to struggle to establish his business. Although he hadn't come to me for marriage counseling, we started discussing his relationship with Marie. I pointed out that the closeness he had enjoyed during their early marriage seemed to have been replaced by a dull flatness. I suggested we also work on some goals and plans for his marriage. He said, "I'm amazed, Doc! I never thought about setting goals for my marriage like I do for my business!" He mentioned somewhat sheepishly that before he was married he used to "romance" his wife, as he put it, but it had been years since they had done anything spontaneous or romantic.

After considerable discussion, we decided to start with a few simple plans to implement his newfound goals of putting some romance back into the marriage. I suggested starting with the easiest plans to achieve. He decided to buy a supply of "love message" cards for his wife and mail her one from time to time. He told me they had dutifully celebrated their anniversary on June sixteenth every year. So as an additional plan I suggested they celebrate an "anniversary" on the sixteenth of every month. Finally, I suggested he take her out to dinner more often, just the two of them, without the kids.

Some of you may be thinking, "Well, there's very little spontaneity in those plans. Aren't those the sort of things he should think of on his own?" Sure they are. But the answer is that if I had left it up to him, he might never have thought of them spontaneously! This way, once he got started on this program, his wife was so pleased that she began to cook special dishes he liked and do other little thoughtful things the way she had done early in their marriage. He told me happily, "We're beginning to live with a kind of 'zing' I'd forgotten about." Incidentally, as his marriage relationship began to change, he was also making a great deal of progress in his business relationships. Creativity in one area often helps in another.

That most people have no goals or plans is unfortunate but not surprising, since the whole concept is a neglected area in our culture. Many people just exist from day to day, week to week, year to year. Others have goals but they are so vague or passive they are virtually worthless. Often I refer to these as "money goals." They want a new Porsche, a trip to Europe, or a mink coat. Fine. Who doesn't? But to achieve such goals you need the money to pay for them. On this point, the person is usually quite vague and has no plan about how to get such a sum of money.

There are some people who "kind of" have goals but they are still in their unconscious mind, vague, and undefined. These people have never taken the time to sit down and pinpoint the specific objectives of their lives.

Still other people have goals that are impossible to obtain. One of my former patients, Bruce, had as his goal an early retirement at age thirty-five. Since he was unable to do this, it had ruined his whole thirty-fifth birthday celebration. Obviously, this was an unrealistic goal, in spite of the fact that this bright young man was highly successful in the business world. How many people are able to retire by the age of thirty-five? And on what? And why? In Bruce's case he had no particular notion of what he wanted to do after retirement. Retirement was his whole goal, rather than it being somehow related to the rest of his life. If he had actually retired at thirty-five, he would have discovered it to be an empty achievement. This man's goal was not only unrealistic; it was incomplete.

Now I want to teach you how to develop meaningful goals, how to define them clearly, and how to create definite plans for reaching them.

So far I have tried to give you a glimpse of the potentialities which exist within you. I have tried to show you your Repressive Self and its defense mechanisms in action, preventing you from becoming the "you" that could be. You have some experiments and exercises which can put you in touch with parts of your Potential Self. But without the ability to formulate goals and plans you would be greatly handicapped in realizing your Potential, even though the desire may exist as a tantalizing possibility. Or you may have goals, but they are so vague that they are useless. Or you may have an impossible goal, such as achieving full use of your Potential Self in six months.

All right, the next step: What will be *your* goals and plans? First, let's go back to the three basic types of Repressive Self. If you have recognized yourself as an appeaser, your goal may be to gradually learn to stand up for yourself. If you recognized yourself as a retreater, your goal may be to get over your fear of people and to allow yourself to become emotionally involved. If you recognized yourself as an aggressor, your goal may be to learn to get satisfactions from other things in life than success.

Since I do not know you personally, I cannot suggest your particular goals, nor can I possibly know what unique and specific potentialities are presently locked inside you by your Repressive Self. But at least I can suggest areas and relationships in which you may set goals.

First, there is the area of your work. You may have many goals in mind here, including "money goals," such as travel, a new house, a new car, or college for your children. The place you are most likely to achieve these money goals is in your world of work.

There is the area of your marriage. Setting goals in this area may head off divorce in the future, or deepen an already satisfactory relationship.

There is the area of children. Most parents have relatively few goals and plans for their children. Like firemen, they rush around putting out daily fires and are too busy to set long-term goals and plans. These parents are missing a great deal in their emotional relationships with their children by not thinking about the future direction the children may take.

If you are not married, then you may be concerned to set goals and plans so that you can find and marry someone with whom you can achieve a happy and lasting relationship. As someone has commented: "Most people put more time and care into choosing a new car than into choosing the right person to spend the rest of their life with."

Finally, there is the whole area of friends. I indicated in the previous chapter how superficial relationships are with "friends" in today's culture. You may want to set some goals and plans here.

Did mentioning these areas stimulate anything in your mind? Do you already have some goals in mind, or did you get a new idea or two? Obviously, this is worth putting some thoughtful time into. Consider these things as you go about the routine tasks of the day—think about your work and its rewards; the quality of your home life, of your marriage, of your relationships with your children, or your friends. Think about your children's future. Think about your own day-to-day existence. Be imaginative as you consider these aspects of your life and how you could change or augment them. Let your creative mind be fanciful; think up far-out ideas. Rediscover your dreams.

At some point in this process, perhaps in a day or somewhat longer, you will be ready for specific planning. This is the most important step—taking specific action on your thoughts.

Find a half-hour when you will be free of all distractions. Use it to make a list of the previous goals you have thought of plus any new ones that occur to you. Include the most outrageous goals you can imagine. Don't worry about whether your ideas are realistic or unrealistic at this point; just write them down. After you have noted all your goals, go over the list carefully and pick out the five which are the most important to you. You may find this a very exciting process.

Your next step is to determine how to reach each of these five goals. Here's where most people go astray because they start out with a plan that is much too ambitious. When it can't be achieved right away, they get discouraged and give up. These are the people who have not learned the lesson of the teaching machine.

Even though many of you have heard the phrase "teaching machine," you may not be familiar with the manner in which it works or the psychological principles on which it is based. (The "brother" of the teaching machine, the programmed book, is a teaching machine in book form, based on exactly the same principles.) The teaching machine or programmed book is planned so that the learner starts out answering very easy questions. He cannot go on to the next question until he has successfully answered the previous one. Finally, at the end of the program or book, the learner is answering very hard questions. The teaching machine or programmed book is constructed so that the student will be successful right from the beginning.

Let the teaching machine be your model. First you write down your goal; your second job is to break your goal into a series of steps, beginning with steps which are absurdly easy. For example, I had a former patient, Max, forty-six years old, who was really out of shape physically. One of his goals was to get back into good physical shape. When I asked him how he planned to do this, Max named a gym—the most expensive in the area—and told me he was going to sign up for its full physical fitness program. He planned to swim twenty laps in the club's pool each morning on his way to work and stop by on the way home each evening to work out on their machines. I immediately realized that this was too elaborate a program and that he would last only a few weeks and then quit.

I suggested we use the teaching machine approach instead. He liked the idea of jogging, so we agreed he should begin by jogging around his house and yard a mere three minutes a day. He wanted to do sit-ups to improve his stomach muscles. We decided he begin by doing only *one* sit-up a day for the first week. Starting with this very easy program, of course, he was successful. Little by little, over a period of five months, he worked up to jogging half an hour and doing fifty sit-ups each morning.

When you are designing a step-by-step plan to achieve your goal, whatever it is, think of my patient and his physical fitness program. Make your first steps to your goal absurdly easy so that you are sure to succeed. Then gradually increase them. Don't rush.

Thinking of Max and his physical fitness program brings to mind Janet, another former patient. Janet had been reducing off and on for years. She must have gained, lost, and regained the same twenty-five pounds at least a dozen times. What she really wanted to do was to lose weight and make sure it stayed off. When we discussed her goal, she realized that in the past she had lost a lot of weight quickly on a crash diet, but then regained it just as quickly.

Janet had been doing a lot of reading about weight control, and she realized she would have a better chance of keeping the weight off if she lost it more slowly. After some discussion, she decided to try to lose one-half pound a week. Since it takes 3,500 calories less than your normal diet to lose a pound a week, Janet needed to eat only 250 calories less each day in order to lose one-half pound a week. This was not an impossible task. And to make it easier, she set up a reward system for herself. Since she was paid every two weeks at her job, she marked on her calendar the weight she expected to be on each payday for the next six months. (That is, one pound lighter than she had been the previous pay period.) If she *was* a pound lighter, she bought herself an inexpensive present (as long as it wasn't food!). Rewarding herself for accomplishing her goal at each stage proved to be the added incentive she needed. For the first time in her life she not only lost the weight, but she did not gain it back again.

Another example explores an entirely different area of human relationships. A thirty-two-year-old woman patient, Ellen, was overwhelmed by feelings of isolation after her divorce. Her goal was to get back into the world of social relationships, but she was terribly afraid of being rejected. I suggested a plan in several steps. First, she was to apply for membership in Parents Without Partners, but she was *not* to go to any of the activities the first month. In fact, she was instructed not even to read the monthly newsletter, listing the various activities. The second month she was to read the newsletter but not to attend any activities. The third month she was to participate in one discussion group only. The fourth month she was to go to two discussion groups. Finally, the fifth month she was to attend a dance. It worked. With each succeeding month and each succeeding step she built up the courage to try the next step of the plan.

Some of these early steps may sound so slow that they don't make sense, and you may feel "nothing is happening." Wrong! Something *is* happening, but it isn't particularly obvious. What is taking place is that your Potential Self is getting into gear for the eventual achievement of your goal. Often your goal is something you would have accomplished already, if some repressive mechanism inside you had not interfered. In addition to guaranteeing success at each step by going slowly at first, you are allowing your sincere desire for the goal to start directing your actions.

Some people, in working toward a goal, find themselves seized by inertia when it comes time for action. If this should happen to you, despite the small graduated steps, then it is time to reexamine your goal. Consider how important it actually is and then either discard the goal (and replace it with a more suitable one) or continue the steps with a renewed sense of the value of achieving it.

When you have chosen your first five goals, be sure to give your unconscious mind a chance to help plan the steps to make them work. With both your conscious and unconscious mind working on the problem, you will be making the best use of your creative mental resources.

My suggestion on how you can best accomplish the planning stage is to write, in brief form on three-by-five cards, the five goals and any steps to achieve them. Tape one of these cards to your mirror where you can see it every day. Put the second one in your pocket or purse. This way you will be thinking daily, both consciously and unconsciously, of these five goals and the steps by which you can achieve them. I do not mean for you to fret and stew, pressuring yourself to come up immediately with the "right way" to achieve them. Just think about them consciously from time to time as you go about your normal routine. At the same time, your unconscious will be doing its work. Your unconscious will usually contribute its part at some unexpected time, such as when you are eating lunch or playing tennis. When this happens, jot down the idea as soon as you can.

For the most part, I am talking about practical, attainable goals. If you happen to choose a long-range endeavor, such as becoming a doctor, you will need to break it down into many, many steps leading to it.

It is important, of course, to be realistic about goals. If you are fifty years old, it is not very realistic to decide to become a doctor. If you are twenty-two it may be. First determine that you have the intellectual equipment and emotional stamina for the job. Get a professional evaluation of this before committing yourself to the goal.

Some goals may be realistic when you set them, but life changes. Do not delude yourself into thinking that everything is standing still while you are moving toward your goals. Your goal may be to improve your marriage relationship, but while you are working toward this, your wife starts action for divorce. Your goal may be to become president of your company. But a new scientific discovery suddenly creates the possibility of a new manufacturing division within your company structure. You realize that your real rewards lie in directing that new division rather than the entire firm. It is important that you not think of either your goals or your plans to achieve them as unalterable and carved in white marble. Goals are made to be shifted and plans are made to be changed. You have not "failed" if you shift a goal or change a plan, whether the choice was yours or not.

197

A goal is an ideal, then, and something entirely outside of your control may force you to lower your sights. Realistically speaking, you may be able to achieve only 25 percent of the goal you originally set. But remember, if you had not set it, you would not have achieved even that 25 percent.

For example, you may have the goal of getting your children to take a more active part in doing chores around the house. You construct a set of plans to involve them in these activities. But after considerable effort on your part and theirs, they are still doing only about 50 percent of the chores you would like. It looks as if things are not going to improve any further, no matter what you try. Then it may be wise for you to accept the 50 percent as the most they are able to do and congratulate them and yourself for the improvements they have made.

Some goals are ideals you will want to continue striving for in spite of difficulties. But when a goal no longer seems realistic, it is best to turn your attention to other goals. A goal should never be used as a perfectionistic standard that forces you to call yourself a "failure" if you do not achieve it 100 percent.

Remember the concept of a baseball player's batting average. A player who bats .300 is considered an excellent hitter. That means he gets three hits out of every ten trips to the plate. Try to allow yourself the same kind of margin with your goals and plans. Don't demand that you bat 1.000 with your goals. Perfection, after all, is not very "human."

If you do the things outlined in this chapter, I can practically guarantee you will be more successful in your life than most people. You will have defined your goals clearly, five at a time. You may not achieve all of every goal, but you will achieve at least part of each.

Be sure to use the model of the teaching machine in programming your plans to achieve your goals. Always begin with ridiculously easy plans at first. This not only helps to start you off, but also to begin it successfully. It is likely you will continue to be successful as you advance from easier plans to harder ones.

Above all, be flexible. Do not hesitate to change either a goal or the plan leading up to it at any time. Do not let your goals run you. You run your goals. After all, you are not trying to add pressures and burdens to your life; you are adding focus.

But be careful not to let yourself slip into the situation where your goals concern only your business or making money. Think of your marriage, your children, and your friends as important areas in which to improve your life.

I have suggested you start by choosing five goals, which is a reasonable number to focus on. Obviously you are not going to keep those same five goals forever. One of two things will happen. As you reach a goal, you will cross it off your list and replace it with a new one; or you will realize that a particular goal is no longer desirable or realistic, and you will adjust or replace it. And so you will go through your life, achieving, adjusting, or discarding goals and replacing them with new ones. In contrast to most people, who let their lives just "go along," your life will always be focused on specific goals with specific plans for achieving them. You will be "on the move" in all important areas of your life with a steady, consistent pace. You will be improving your situation and increasing your happiness.

By use of specific goals and plans you will be getting rid of your Repressor and actualizing your Potential Self.

10: *If You Need Professional Help*

As some of you try to put into practice the teachings and exercises of this book, you may run into emotional snags that make it difficult, or even impossible, to do so. You may discover that your Repressive Self is too strong and too deeply engrained in your personality, and you are not able to achieve the results you want entirely by your own efforts. Or, on the other hand, as you try some of the exercises, you may find yourself flooded with feelings of anxiety or other uncomfortable signals of psychological distress. Do not interpret this as a sign of weakness.

It may mean that you need professional assistance in breaking loose from your Repressive Self and discovering your Potential Self.

People often ask, "How do I know if I need psychological help?" My answer is, if it even enters your mind that you may need psychological help, then go for one consultation and see how you feel about it.

On the first consultation, people often say, "I'm not sure I should even be here. Maybe I don't need psychological help at all." Such thinking is a holdover from the old days when a person felt great shame in getting help for emotional problems. He felt he must be "weak" or have a "defect of character" if he could not solve all of his problems without getting outside assistance. Although this opinion has changed considerably, remnants of it still exist.

People often tell me "I picked up the phone to make an appointment with you; then I put it down. I asked myself 'Should I do this, or should I give it one more try on my own?' I picked up the phone again, started to dial, and put it down again. Finally, I went ahead and made the call." I usually point out to this person that if he had a broken leg and was phoning a physician, he would never go through this kind of one-act drama. He would simply pick up the phone and make an appointment to get the broken leg taken care of as soon as possible. The reason he would call so easily and straightforwardly is that our culture has not attached any shame or connotations of moral failure to getting professional help for a broken leg.

Far from thinking of it as a sign of shame or moral failure, we would consider this decision a mark of wisdom, intelligence, and enlightenment.

The fact is, you do not necessarily need to have trouble in accomplishing the teachings and exercises of this book to profit by professional help in finding your Potential Self. You can get the equivalent of a college education in a public library, but it is easier to get it in a college or university where you have skilled teachers to guide you. In the same way, you will find it easier to break the hold of your Repressive Self and get in touch with the untapped resources of your Potential Self with the aid of a skilled professional person.

All right then. Let's suppose for one reason or another you decide to seek professional assistance. How do you go about it?

Let me begin by warning you what *not* to do. Throughout the country there are groups which meet on a one-time basis, usually for a weekend, variously known as "encounter groups," "growth groups," and so forth. Some of these may be ongoing groups which meet once a week. Some are led by well-trained, qualified professionals in the field of mental health: psychologists, psychiatrists, and psychiatric social workers. These groups usually help the people who participate.

Unfortunately, some groups are led by untrained people—usually *not* psychologists, psychiatrists, or psychiatric social workers. Since the law forbids them to use these professional names, they often call themselves "psychotherapists." Apparently there is no law forbidding anyone to call himself a psychotherapist. If you are interested in joining such a group (particularly on the glowing recommendation of a friend), find out the following information about its leader: Is he a psychiatrist, psychologist, or psychiatric social worker? If not, be suspicious. Find out what degree he holds, from what university or medical school, and how many years of experience he has had in the field of psychotherapy. You would be amazed at the number of people attending "encounter groups" led by "psychotherapists" whose backgrounds make them totally unqualified.

Although I am a firm believer in the power of group therapy, I am generally very skeptical of a single weekend group and thoroughly suspicious if the leader is a nonprofessional. In my opinion, to be effective, a group needs to be ongoing and meet weekly. Very few psychological miracles are wrought in one weekend.

Almost all of us who have been in clinical practice for some time have seen patients who were badly scarred emotionally as the result of attending one of these weekend groups. Two examples come to mind. One was a young man who came to me as a patient after such a weekend experience. The group leader told him he was "probably a latent homosexual." No life history background, no psychological testing on which to base such a judgment! And even if it were true, the psychological crudity of making such an interpretation after seeing the man for only two hours! He was left to sink or swim—the group leader did not care to take responsibility for the consequences of the authoritative judgment he had so glibly pronounced.

A married woman was told at such a weekend group that she needed to have an affair. She was very insecure about many aspects of her life at this time and was unable to evaluate realistically for herself the advice she had been given. Unfortunately, she followed the advice of this group and its leader and ended up in the divorce court when her husband found out.

These are the kind of shoot-from-the-hip, anything-goes interpretations that people are likely to get at groups with untrained leaders. Give these kinds of encounter groups a wide berth.

How do you find a good therapist for yourself for individual or group therapy? First of all, as I mentioned before, there are only three professions and some members of a fourth who will have the training and experience you need: psychologists, psychiatrists, psychiatric social workers, and occasionally a minister with psychological training. In theory at least, all members of these professions should be adequately qualified to help you. How do you find them? You may get names from your family doctor, your minister, or your local psychological or psychiatric association. You can also look up names under psychologists or physicians (those who specialize in psychiatry) in the Yellow Pages of your local telephone directory. Sometimes you can get the names of professionals in the mental health field from a local help line.

There are two main ways to find a therapist these days. Someone (a physician, minister, or friend) refers you to a particular therapist. Or you turn to the Yellow Pages and pick blindly. The point is that people usually go to the first therapist they contact. I think this may turn out to be a potential mistake.

Instead of continuing with the first therapist you visit, I suggest you make appointments with three therapists. Invest the time and money to talk with each one for an hour. I think you will find it worthwhile. Ask about his educational background. What degree does he hold and from which university or medical school? Where did he do his internship, and at what mental hospital or mental hygiene clinics has he worked? How many years has he been in practice? These are, in a sense, the "technical" questions. You must remember that a therapist could have adequate training and background and still be a poor therapist. Or he could be a reasonably good therapist for some other patient, but a poor therapist for you.

You are going to spend a lot of time with your therapist after you choose him, and it is extremely important that the "vibes" be good on both sides. If you take the trouble to make this initial survey, your chances of finding a good therapist will be considerably improved. Whether the therapist should be a psychiatrist, a psychologist, a psychiatric social worker, or a psychologically trained minister is immaterial. What is important is how well you and he can relate emotionally.

Perhaps you are presently considering the use of professional assistance in freeing your Potential

Self. But you may be thinking "I just can't afford to see a therapist in private practice—the fees are too high." First of all, check and see if your particular insurance policy will cover this type of therapy. An increasing number of companies are presently paying a portion of this kind of medical expense.

If this resource is not available, and if you live in a reasonably large city, you will usually find several low-cost psychological clinics where the fees are based on a sliding scale, according to the ability to pay. One of the problems is that the waiting list is usually long. But if you really want therapy, you can get it if you are patient and persistent.

If you live in a small town or rural area far from any kind of mental health facilities, there is no easy answer. Unfortunately, it is true that physical health facilities are much more available than mental health facilities. You may have to drive long distances to get the therapy you need. Or perhaps as one of your goals you could join with other people and help bring mental health facilities to your area!

In summary, you may decide for one of several reasons you need professional help to achieve the goals outlined in this book. First, you may find that your Repressive Self is too strong and deeply engrained for you to do the job by yourself. Or you may decide it will be easier and faster to achieve your goals with professional assistance.

Some form of professional guidance is available. Don't hesitate to get it if it will benefit you.

Epilogue

Good luck in your journey toward self-actualization! I have tried to present as clear and straightforward an account as I can of your Repressive Self and its defense mechanisms and your Potential Self and its great potentialities.

Since a book is unfortunately a one-way conversation and we do not have an opportunity to talk back and forth in person, I invite your questions and comments. There may be comments you wish to make about the book, things you disagree with, or questions you want to ask about things I didn't deal with in the book. You can write to me in care of my publisher, Follett Publishing Company.